HEALING FOR GOD'S WORLD

HEALING FOR GOD'S WORLD

Remedies from
Three Continents

Kofi Asare Opoku
Kim Yong-Bock
Antoinette Clark Wire

Friendship Press • **New York**

Library of Congress Cataloging in Publication Data

Healing for God's world : remedies from three continents / Kofi Asare
   Opoku, Kim Yong-Bock, Antoinette Clark Wire.
     p.   cm.
   "The Joseph Cook lectureship...seventh"—P. vii.
   Includes bibliographical references.
   ISBN 0-377-00229-1
   1. Theology–20th century. 2. Progress–Religious aspects—
Christianity. 3. Wealth, Ethics of. I. Opoku, Kofi Asare.
II. Kim, Yong-bok, 1938-   III. Wire, Antoinette Clark. IV. Title:
Joseph Cook lectureship.
BT28.H335   1991
261—dc20   91-2154
                                       CIP

CONTENTS

THE JOSEPH COOK
LECTURESHIP

Joseph Cook, eminent lecturer, writer, and Christian apologist, who died in 1901, left his estate in trust to the Presbyterian Board of Foreign Missions, the income to be devoted to a lectureship, "to be filled by Christian scholars in defense of Christianity, who shall be chosen by the Board, and visit in succession the principal cities of China, India and Japan."

In 1924, the Rev. Cleland B. McAfee, D.D., was appointed the first Cook lecturer; the second was the Rev. J. Harry Cotton, D.D., in 1931. The third Cook lecturer, in 1946–47, was the Rev. Henry Sloane Coffin, D.D. In 1951–52, the Rev. George A. Buttrick, D.D., and in 1960–61 Dr. John A. Mackay were the Cook lecturers. Dr. C. S. Song and Dr. Gayraud Wilmore were the lecturers in 1971 under the joint sponsorship of the East Asia Christian Conference and the Commission on Ecumenical Mission and Relations.

The seventh Cook Lectureship was carried out as an ecumenical team. Three outstanding Christian theologians, Prof. Kim Yong-Bock of Korea, Prof. Kofi Asare Opoku of Ghana, and Prof. Antoinette Clark Wire of the United States joined together in giving a series of lectures in various countries of Asia and in the U.S.A. on "Responses in Faith to Broken Humanity: Contributions from Three Continents."

A word of special thanks is due L. Newton Thurber for his vision and guidance in moving the contributions of these fine theologians from lecture to print.

FOREWORD

Throughout the twentieth century the Joseph Cook Lectureships have engaged some of the most prominent and articulate American Christian scholars in lecturing "in defense of Christianity" in various parts of Asia. The lecturers have included well-known preachers and teachers such as Henry Sloane Coffin, George Buttrick, and John Mackay.

The latest Cook Lectureship, which occurred in 1988, drew on three scholars who come from backgrounds and traditions different from those who have been selected throughout most of the history of the lectureship. These scholars are:

- Kofi Asare Opoku, a Ghanaian scholar in the field of African religion.

- Kim Yong-Bock, a Korean *minjung* theologian and human rights activist.

- Antoinette Clark Wire, an American feminist New Testament professor.

Rather than give the lectures only in Asia, as has been the custom, the 1988 lectures were given both in various parts of Asia but also in various parts of the United States.

These shifts in tradition represent more than changes in the sex and/or ethnicity of the lecturers. They also reflect profound theological shifts and a changing understanding of the global Christian community. They attempt to give expression to the recognition that Christian theology is not primarily a European and North American enterprise to be shared with the rest of the world. It is rather an enterprise of the global Christian community that is to be shared between and among all six continents. In this enterprise the

9

voices from "the underside of history" seem to be the ones with the most vitality and the most provocative messages to the global Christian community. The Cook lecturers of 1988 demonstrate that reality in a remarkable way in the five lectures that follow.

Healing for God's World: Remedies from Three Continents is a publication of five of the lectures given during the Cook Lectureship of 1988. They have been published by Friendship Press because of the extremely positive response to the lectures and the desire to share them with a wider audience. They have also been published because they address issues that are absolutely crucial to the future of Christian witness as well as the future of the world.

This book is being published at a time in which the theme ("Healing for God's World") could not be more timely. As I write this foreword, the evidences of the brokenness of our world are almost overwhelming:

- The world stands on a verge of a major military conflagration in the Persian Gulf.

- Troops are crushing the hopes for freedom in Lithuania and the Baltic states.

- War and enforced starvation threaten the very fabric of human life in Sudan, Somalia, and Liberia.

- The recession in the United States means growing homelessness, increased despair, and a growing rate of incarceration (already the highest in the world) among the poor.

The authors remind us that if God is the creator, all people are the people of God and have a right to live as people created in the image of God. They also remind us that God acts for the liberation of those who live on the "underside of history" and that faithful witness to the gospel requires a struggle to insure the full humanity of all human beings envisioned in Jesus Christ. They remind those of us in the church that we have been called to be healers of God's broken world and open to remedies that the Holy Spirit may be bringing to us through the weak and wounded of the earth. This volume is an excellent resource for those committed through faith in Jesus Christ to be involved in the ministry of healing God's broken world.

In this volume Kofi Opoku develops these themes from the perspective of African culture and its encounter with the gospel. He connects the unique strengths of African communalism with the message of *koinonia* in the gospel. He suggests that that linkage can empower the search for community against the powerful forces that destroy community in our world today: threats to cultural identity, economic exploitation, the arms buildup, environmental destruction, and racism and apartheid. He uses the fascinating image from African traditional religion of a "Siamese crocodile," which has two heads and two tails but a common stomach. He reminds us that our world has many heads and many tails but that we should never forget that we all have a "common stomach."

In his second essay he relates the concepts of salvation in African traditional religion with the wholistic understanding of salvation found in the biblical record. He indicates that both point to the same urgent need for Christian theology (especially that which has originated in the West) to move from a notion of salvation centered on redemption from sin and guilt to a wholistic understanding of salvation that offers genuine hope for the healing of all the pains and divisions of our broken world.

Kim Yong-Bock, doing theology in the context of the struggle of the people (*minjung*) in Korea, addresses issues that are key to the healing of our world. He reclaims economics as a concern for theology and for the human future. In the midst of principalities and powers represented in the worldwide technocratic penetration of the economic system and in superpower control of world politics, he calls for a political economy of the people of God. He finds biblical resources for this concept in the liberation of the slaves through the Exodus and in the political economy of the early church. He also finds illustrations in the history of the suffering people of Korea (the *minjung*) and in the basic premises of *Minjung* theology, i.e., that people are the subject of history and that ultimate power is found in the suffering love of Christ. Such a vision of politics and economics calls for a deep faith in the power of people's movements and a strong commitment to challenge the principalities and powers that control the economic and political systems of our world.

Antoinette Clark Wire provides biblical, and especially New Testament, resources for the struggle for the healing of this broken world. Her first essay reclaims a theology of power from the accounts of the miracles of Jesus. She shows that through the miracle stories run the following themes: the celebration of the struggle against evil; the challenge to those afflicted by evil to claim the power to be human; the dramatization of the right to be well and whole. She illustrates how this theology of power growing out of the miracle stories has been reclaimed by Chinese Christians in recent years. She further argues that the miracles should play a far greater role in Christian theology if we are serious about the healing of the world.

Her second essay on the Corinthian women prophets provides a fascinating insight into the power of the Spirit in the "non-writers" of the New Testament. She shows how the Corinthian women prophets, who were subject of Paul's admonition to silence and submission, understood far better than the apostle himself the depth and power of his affirmation, "There is no longer Jew or Greek, there is no longer slave or free, there is no longer male or female; for all of you are one in Christ Jesus" (Gal. 3:28). She points out that this experience illustrates that people from different social positions often find different ways of expressing the Christian faith and that those who are on the lower end of the scale of human power often have the deepest insights into the truth and power of the gospel.

Together these five essays provide important theological resources for a ministry of healing the world in which we live. If we truly believe that God is indeed the creator, redeemer, and sustainer of the world, there can be no more important task for the Christian churches as we move toward the twenty-first century. In the Worldwatch Institute's most recent report, *The State of the World: 1990,* the authors concluded, "Only a monumental effort can reverse the deterioration of the planet."[1] These five essays give Christians resources and vision to tackle that monumental calling.

Professors Opoku, Kim, and Wire approach the question of healing the world from different perspectives, differing life histories, differing socio-political contexts, and different academic disciplines. However, they point to a common hope of a new order of humanity in Christ. That new order of humanity stands in stark contrast to the current exploitation of our planet, to the politics of oppression, to the economics of domination, and to the subjugation of so many based on race and sex. Theirs is a message that both the churches and the world need to hear!

CLIFTON KIRKPATRICK

---

[1]Lester R. Brown, *State of the World: 1990* (New York: W.W. Norton & Company, 1990), xv.

1

IN PURSUIT OF COMMUNITY: AN AFRICAN PERSPECTIVE

Kofi Asare Opoku

We live in a severely fragmented world. More than forty years ago, with the carnage and indescribable destruction of the Second World War fresh in the minds of people the world over, humankind resolved to create a better, more harmonious, and more just world. It seemed then that there was a genuine desire among the nations to come together to work for a peaceful world in which mutual discussion rather than war would be the means of solving international problems. The United Nations was born in 1945 with fifty-one nations coming together to build a better future; with the process of decolonization that accelerated after the Second World War, its membership has now risen to 159. Concern with human rights was given concrete expression in the adoption of the United Nations Charter of Human Rights, and strenuous efforts were made to create better trade relations among the nations of the world.

But in the years after the end of the Second World War, a war which was fought, so it was believed, to end all wars, the world, especially the countries of the South — in Africa, Asia, the Middle East, Latin American, and the Caribbean — has experienced over one hundred wars, which have resulted in the death of thirty million people, more than half the total number of deaths recorded during the Second World War.[1] And while there has been no war in America or Europe during this period, it hardly needs pointing out that American and European political, economic, and financial institutions have played a not inconsiderable role in promoting and perpetuating conditions of conflict in the South.

Increasingly, international consensus, which the United Nations hoped to buttress, has been on the wane, and the decisions that affect the entire world have progressively been taken by a handful of highly industrialized countries that have assumed the right to decide the fate of other peoples of the world. This trend is evidenced by the economic summit conferences of the industrial and economic giants of the world, that have been held since 1976. These giants look after their own interests, and rational selfishness seems to be the order of the day.

The gap between the rich nations and the poor ones continues to widen. The rich nations tend to be concentrated in the North and the poor ones in the South, although there are pockets of poverty in the North as well as pockets of wealth in the South. But on the whole, the South is economically exploited by the rich North, and there is a growing indifference to the ever-widening gap between the North and the South. When it is borne in mind that the North, which has a quarter of the world's population, enjoys four-fifths of the world's income, while the South, including China, has three-quarters of the world's population but enjoys only one-fifth of the world's income,[2] then the injustice in the present-day world economic order becomes self-evident, and one cannot fail to see that the conditions that lead to conflict and strife are present in this gross state of inequality.

The polarization of the world into East and West, with its attendant big-power rivalry, has further worsened conditions in an already fragmented and increasingly violent world. The greatest threat to world peace comes from the utterly absurd and insane arms race, which not only increases the danger of nuclear war and destruction of the whole world but also diverts attention and much-needed resources from the solution of the pressing problems facing humankind. But the poor countries, which can ill afford it, are as much involved in the craze for arms and maintenance of armed forces as are the rich countries.

Racism continues to play an increasingly prominent

role in accentuating the divisions in the world today. Related to this is the noticeable and alarming growth of provincialism and palpably narrower perspectives, which diminish the internationalism that characterized the world during the period immediately following the Second World War. Increasingly, immigration rules are being tightened, especially for nonwhites, in countries whose populations are predominantly of European extraction, and nonwhites often experience humiliation at ports of entry into predominantly white countries. The resultant anger, resentment, and frustration further accentuate the divisions.

The depth and variety of the divisions that militate against the achievement of unity among the people of the world must be a source of urgent concern for Christians committed to doing the will of God. As a World Council of Churches' study stated:

> Christians begin their reflection on community from the acknowledgment that God as they believe Him to have come in Jesus Christ is the Creator of all things and of all humankind; that from the beginning He willed a relationship with Himself and between all that He has brought to life; that to that end He has enabled the formation of communities, judges them and renews them.[3]

If the claim of the church to be the body of Christ is to have any meaning whatever, then it is to be seen in how Christians individually and collectively respond to the challenges they face in the world today, in how they bring healing and wholeness into human lives, in how they enable human beings to live creatively as children of God, and in how they awaken a profoundly concrete appreciation of the living reality who is God.

Merely living next to each other does not signify community, for the proper foundation of community is fellowship, sharing, and familyhood. A common purpose that involves a shared transcendent image of human living gives meaning to true community.

It is important to bear in mind that the divisions in our world today seem to overshadow the basic underlying unity that should characterize and hold together humankind. We all, human beings and all other created things, participate in one life whose only source is God, and, as Paul reminds us, God has made the earth and all the nations of the earth of one blood. Furthermore, the Christian covenant in the blood and the body of Christ unites us with Christ. The one bread in which we share forms us into one body. "So we, though many, are one body in Christ, and individually members one of another" (Rom. 12:5).[4] The pursuit of a community of all God's children is a striving for the values of the reign of God. As Mercy Oduyoye puts it:

> Let us live our lives before the one God whose will is that the human community should conform to the values of the kingdom of God. When we are able to do this then we can begin to appreciate the implications of baptism and the Eucharist as sacraments building up not only our community with one another as human beings but also with God in whose image we are made and whose name is engraved on our hearts.[5]

The community we seek is one in which all narrow limits are widened until community embraces the whole world, *oikoumene*, the total inhabited world. And as part of our faith commitment, we need to face the challenge to relativize our parochial and national loyalties.[6] For it is only when we live as a community that we can enjoy full blessedness: sharing with others in a common purpose, namely, that we were made for God and not for ourselves. The pursuit of community is also a search for a new way forward. As John Pobee writes: "In practical terms it means religious people helping to find a new economic, industrial and commercial order that matches, if not flows out of, the Christian perception of human nature and destiny."[7]

THE AFRICAN EXPERIENCE OF COMMUNITY

The most important characteristic of community in Africa is wholeness, for the community is made up not only of the living. There is an extrahuman dimension or religious foundation to the community, because it goes beyond the limits of its visible members to include others who are not visible: God, the Overlord of the community; the ancestors, or living-dead, who are forbears and predecessors of the community and who uphold communal unity and cooperation; the divinities and spirits; and those who are yet to be born.

Traditional education gives primary place to personal relations, and to be human is to be in relation not only with the visible human members of one's family, clan, or community, but also with the spiritual beings in the community as well as with nature. The importance of relationship lies in the fact that each person shares familyhood in common with all others, and the community is therefore an integrated entity that is undergirded and kept alive by extended relationships, the purpose of which is to enhance unity and promote greater friendly cooperation.

Mutual helpfulness, cooperation, generosity, complementarity, and interdependence are the key principles in the organization of the community. Individuals therefore see their neighbor as their other arm and not as their competitor. This relationship is expressed in the Akan proverb *Nifa guare benkum, na benkum guare nifa* (The right arm washes the left and the left also washes the right). And when this happens, both arms become clean. The emphasis on cooperation, mutual helpfulness, concern for the welfare of the group as virtues fundamental to the community ideal is based on the assumption that life's meaning is realized more fully when an individual is a member of a group or community.

The relationship of the individual to the community is expressed by saying, "I am because we are, and because we are, therefore I am." This gives eloquent expression to the African view that life's purposes and aims can be brought to consummation when an individual is part of the group and not when a person lives a state of isolated individualism. Being a part of the community does not mean that the individual's interest is sacrificed to group interest, for the well-being of the community cannot be considered in isolation from that of the individual. In the

African view of things, the needs and interests of all the individual members of the community can best be taken care of by a system of communalism, which is geared toward the promotion of the general welfare of all who belong to the community.

In the African view, a human being is social by nature and cannot live outside society. Society, therefore, is the context for authentic human existence. An Akan proverb underscores the view that a human being is not born to live a life of solitariness: *Onipa fi soro besi a, obsi wo nnipa krom* (When a person descends from heaven, he or she descends into a town inhabited by human beings [human society]). Human beings are not self-sufficient to the extent that our basic needs can be met singlehandedly. To meet our basic needs, we require the assistance of others, and mutual interdependence is therefore a *sine qua non* of life in community. We need to be in relation with others in order to realize our full personality and potential, and the African tradition firmly maintains that individuals can develop their potential only with the aid of a closely knit community. This view sharply contrasts with the position of Western philosophy that argues that only through the enhancement of individual concerns can the community be benefited.

The acknowledgment that persons require the assistance of others in order to realize their full potential does not amount to a denial of human possibilities; on the contrary, human possibilities are enhanced when they are linked with those of others in community. Cooperation, mutual help, and collective action are necessary for individual welfare, and they make possible undertakings that otherwise appear difficult. An Ibo proverb puts the matter in this way: "If anyone thinks that to go in pairs [cooperate with each other] is not useful, let him hold his upper lip and see whether the lower one can speak alone."

In the art of the Akan people the relationship between the individual and society is symbolized by a Siamese crocodile, with two heads, two tails, and a common stomach. The saying goes that although they have a common stomach, they struggle over food (as if the food were going

into different stomachs). The two heads of the crocodile give expression to the uniqueness and individuality of each member of society. It is because of our individuality, which expresses itself in different choices, tastes, passions, and wishes, that conflicts arise in society. But in spite of these conflicts, the symbol provides the background against which these conflicts should be viewed, and that is the common stomach. Members of the community share an identity of interests, and this common interest requires the cooperation of all. The contribution of each person leads to the good of all, and the symbol eloquently depicts the futility of social conflicts. In fact life is not life at all unless it is shared.

COMMUNITY WITH NATURE

The idea of community is not restricted to relations among human beings in society. In a much larger sense, the human being's life is intimately bound up with nature, which is the irreplaceable basis of life. The human being is part of nature and is expected to cooperate with it; nature is not regarded as "other" but as an integral part of humankind's world order.[8] Quite apart from providing sustenance for human beings, nature provides a model, a source of wisdom for the resolution of conflicts in human society. The relationship with nature is often expressed in terms of identity and kinship, friendliness and respect, and this attitude is based on faith in the goodness of the goal of nature. Use is nevertheless made of nature, even though nature is revered.

Features of the environment are often personified in the African religious heritage; this is a way of relating to nature and keeping a harmonious relationship between human beings and their environment. An African Consultation report has stated:

> Our concept of taboo as a ritual prohibition is designed to protect nature; its violation calls for restitution to be made to nature. Humanity is at the center of the cosmos, not in a self-appointed or self-assertive role, but in a dependent, caretaker role, for its life depends on cosmic harmony being maintained. Nature is therefore not an object but a tangible reality from which humanity derives its sense of wholeness and well-being.[9]

Keeping community with nature also means preserving it. Among fishermen in Ghana, it is demanded by tradition that they "sacrifice" some of their catch from the sea to *Bosompo*, the god of the sea, after each fishing expedition before returning home. The fish that are sacrificed must be live fish, not dead ones, and an Akan maxim that supports this ritual says: *Bosompo ankame wo nam a, wo nso wonkame no abia* (If the god of the sea does not begrudge you this fish, you do not begrudge him your catch). The fish sacrificed to *Bosompo* will continue to breed, and there will continue to be fish in the ocean if this ritual is observed. It is therefore taboo for a fisherman not to make a sacrifice; the concern for the environment expressed in the ritual sacrifice is quite evident.

In the farming areas, too, it is taboo for anyone to bring home a whole bunch of palm fruits from the farm. One is expected by custom to cut off some of the palm fruits and leave the nuts in the forest before returning home. The idea behind this is that every palm fruit that is brought home is going to be boiled or cooked and the kernels will not germinate, but the palm fruits left on the farm or in the forest will germinate and grow into palm trees and provide food not only for the present generation but also for future generations. Those who do not observe this taboo are regarded as a threat to human society and are dealt with accordingly.

The importance of the taboo is not diminished by the argument that squirrels and crows that feed on ripe palm fruits do propagate the seeds and therefore render the taboo of no consequence in "modern" times. Such an argument ignores human responsibility toward the environment inherent in the taboo. It is not the responsibility of squirrels and crows or, for that matter, any other animal to ensure human survival and ecological balance. It is human responsibility, and that is why infringement of the taboo is taken seriously. It is clear that the observance of this taboo is an expression of concern for the environment and its preservation, which contributes to the wholeness of human life.

FORCES DISRUPTIVE OF COMMUNITY

The forces that militate against community in our world today are many and constitute a challenge to Christians everywhere to respond creatively out of faith and not out of parochial and myopic self-interest.

Threats to Cultural Identity

Many people in the world today are faced with a threat to their cultural identity that places their dignity as human beings in jeopardy. A people's dignity cannot be separated from their culture; any attempt to trample upon their culture amounts to trampling upon their souls. Every culture has equal dignity and has something to offer to the world. It is a loss to the entire world if any culture is allowed or is forced by circumstances to be obliterated. For in losing a culture the world sacrifices an important element in its foundation.

Through imperialism, colonialism, and neocolonialism, some cultures have tried to extend themselves at the expense of others The most injurious effect of European colonialism on Africa, for example, was the cultural domination that accompanied it. This led to a questioning of the humanity of Africans and a wounding of the African spirit. As Ngugi wa Thiong'o has written:

> The biggest weapon wielded and actually daily unleashed by imperialism against that collective defiance is the cultural bomb. The effect of a cultural bomb is to annihilate a people's belief in their names, in their language, in their environment, in their heritage of struggle, in their unity, in their capacities and ultimately in themselves. It makes them see their past as one wasteland of nonachievement and it makes them want to distance themselves from that wasteland. It makes them want to identify with that which is furthest removed from themselves; for instance, with other people's languages rather than their own. It makes them identify with that which is decadent and reactionary, all these forces which would stop their own springs of life.[10]

The attempt at cultural domination stemmed from a parochialism that neither appreciated nor respected diversity. It reflected ignorance of the fact that by being open to learning from other cultures people are enabled to develop ways of thinking about themselves and others that are fair and just, the foundation for the much-needed peace and understanding for which our world hungers.

Even Christianity, despite its enormous contributions, was made to play a decisive role in the cultural invasion from Europe. The disdainful and condemnatory attitude of many a missionary to things African, based on a feeling that the missionaries represented a superior culture, led to the negation of the African experience. There was therefore an attempt to Europeanize Africans before Christianizing them; in the process the African spirit was further wounded. Alioune Diop's poignant statement in 1962 still has urgent significance today:

> Because the authority of Western culture and Western institutions outstripped ours where the expression of faith was concerned, it succeeded in converting African Christians into a people without soul or visage, a pale shadow of the dominating pride of the Christian West. At the very heart and center of the church in Africa, we have in fact witnessed the mutilation of the African Personality, and the trampling of human dignity in Africa.[11]

However much cultural erosion has taken place under a combined colonial and missionary effort, Africans still live and breathe African culture and cannot completely move away from their cultural background. And it is this cultural background that enables a people to maintain its identity.

We live in an interdependent world, and no one people can claim to have all the answers to the problems of human existence. An African proverb says: "Wisdom is like a baobab tree, and a single man's hand cannot embrace it." No human group has all the answers, and it is in our greater interest to share unstintingly what we have. In doing so we enrich each other's lives.

Christians need to encourage a self-awareness that buttresses the identity of each people and effectively counters all attempts to undermine their humanity. It is only when people have belief in themselves as children of God and have an attitude of respect and appreciation for themselves and their traditions that the wounds that have been inflicted on them will begin to heal. As the wounds are healed, they will also be freeing those who inflicted them from the limitations of narrow-mindedness and prejudice, unmistakable signs of weakness and sickness that cry for healing. Masao Takenaka's comments have a bearing on this problem:

We are indeed entering a new stage of our pilgrimage in human history; we need to take each basic culture seriously in order to attain the unity of humankind. Local and ethnic cultures cannot be given up for the sake of a national or international culture. In our common pilgrimage, the local and ethnic identity should not be an appendage to national life. It goes beyond national boundaries since it touches something essential and basic to human life. It invites echoes and aspirations of the universal.[12]

Economic Exploitation

The enormous reserves of Africa and most of the countries of the South are exploited to support the countries of the North, especially in the West. This situation began in the colonial days and has persisted up to independence and after. Colonialism introduced cash crops for export to the metropolitan countries, and other products such as minerals and timber were also exploited for export.

The imposed role of primary producer of raw materials has severely crippling consequences. Emphasis in these countries is placed on export crops to the neglect of locally required foodstuffs; fertile lands, which could be made to produce food for local consumption, are made to produce what the people do not need. This leads to insufficient local food production and hunger. The price of the cash crops is determined by the buyers, who always want cheaper prices in order to maximize their profits. Attempts to process raw materials before exporting them are met with resistance and high tariffs, which make the products uncompetitive and force a return to exporting raw produce.

At the same time, the manufactured products that the buyers of the raw products make are sold at exorbitant prices since control of the manufactured products lies in the hands of the manufacturers. On both counts, therefore, countries of the South are at the mercy of those of the North, which are determined to keep their position of advantage. The price of commodities has fallen drastically in recent years; increased prices of manufactured goods have further reduced the purchasing power of the export commodities. For example, 24 tons of raw sugar could buy a sixty horsepower tractor in 1959, but by 1982 it took 115 tons of raw sugar to buy the same tractor, and in 1987 it took 133 tons.

The United Nations Secretary General's Report in 1987 on the United Nations Programme for Economic Recovery and Development provides some staggering facts.[13] It says that commodity prices for Africa plummeted to their lowest levels in thirty years and that total export receipts fell by $19 billion to $46 billion (from $65 billion in 1985). Meanwhile, the prices of imported manufactured goods increased by 20 percent, which resulted in a 1986 deterioration in terms of trade of about 32 percent. This was a massive blow, which even the richest countries could not bear, and yet the economically poor countries of Africa had to bear it.

This unquestionably unjust economic relationship has plunged Africa further and further into crippling poverty and underdevelopment. Export earnings are not enough and are consumed by the high cost of imports; this leads to a huge trade gap that is filled by loans and aid grants. The borrowing of huge sums of money and the increasingly high rates of interest have become one of the major stumbling blocks in Africa's development. While Africa needs all the money it can get to finance much-needed projects, it has to meet its debt obligations and send more and more money out of Africa. This trend has been on the increase since 1981, and in 1985 Africa sent $21.5 billion outside Africa. In the same year, according to a report by the International Monetary Fund, the seven largest borrowers of the Third World — Brazil, Mexico, South Korea, Argentina, Venezuela, Indonesia, and the Philippines — sent $32 billion to their creditors in the North; this figure represented 20 percent of the entire export earnings of these countries.

On the whole, about half of Africa's Gross Domestic Product and nearly three to four times its annual export income, a figure that ranges between $150 and $200 billion, represents Africa's current debt. The servicing of this huge and crippling debt means that in most instances 50 to 100 percent of all income from exports has to go toward servicing the debt, leaving little for essential and pressing needs and robbing the people of minimal life-support systems. And while outside assistance has come in, the extent of the indebtedness and its servicing make its impact rather slight, since more money leaves Africa than comes in.

While it is true that the blame for some of these huge debts rests with profligate politicians, the responsibility to face the problem and deal with it justly and realistically rests on both debtors and creditors. An Akan proverb says, *Obi afom akum a, wonfom ngua* (If someone accidentally kills an animal, you do not accidentally skin it). In other words, if someone makes a mistake you do not worsen it. Creditors have every right to collect their loans, but they should not overburden debtors with demands that take their human dignity from them.

These burning issues do not receive much attention from the church, which focuses on "spiritual" concerns, leaving these hard facts of life to politicians, governments, or international corporations. And yet it is in these areas that the church can demonstrate its concern with justice — economic, social, and political — which is part of its total mission in the world.

The church can demonstrate clearly that no area of human life lies outside God's concern and that in all matters it is the good of God's children that should receive utmost consideration rather than the need for financial or market forces to operate efficiently. Thus Christians should become aware of the socio-economic conditions in which a large segment of humankind lives and strive to search for humane solutions. In the face of the exploitation of resources to the detriment of others, Christians should relentlessly advocate the sharing of resources for the good of all, for all resources belong to God who gave them for the good of all. Sharing the abundant resources of the world to bring dignity to all, as John Pobee rightly points out, requires a "real conversion experience with regard to some of the practices in the international economic order."[14] But the effort must continue to be made for that "conversion experience," because we are all witnesses to the gross injustices and inequalities that have resulted from the "market forces" being left entirely to themselves, as Harold Lever and Christopher Huhne put it, "as if financial markets operate in a vacuum and are not powerfully conditioned by the actions of our great financial institutions."[15]

The call by the Pontifical Commission for Justice and Peace in January 1987 for an ethical approach to the problem of international debt — based on the firm conviction that cooperation that transcends collective selfishness and vested interest could effectively tackle the debt crisis and mark progress along the path of international economic justice — showed much admirable originality in its emphasis on the human and moral dimensions of the problem.[16] The report urges international financiers to show "discernment surpassing criteria of profitability and security of loan capital" and goes on to ask rich countries to assume their "duty of solidarity, modify economic policies which contribute to the growth of inequalities between rich and poor,...renounce protectionist measures limiting developing countries' exports to favor reforms in international trade which would result in a just distribution of the fruits of that growth." The report also calls on multinational corporations to participate in Third World debt alleviation, but its main thrust is that priority must be given to human beings and their needs "above and beyond the constraints and financial mechanisms often advanced as the only imperatives."[17] Such an approach will help considerably to strengthen the idea of a community of nations in our world today.

The Arms Buildup

The arms buildup is the biggest and most serious threat to peace and security and the achievement of a world community in which human beings can live creatively as God's children. All the high-level pronouncements by world leaders regarding their commitment to peace are rendered empty when we bear in mind that at the same time these pronouncements are being made these leaders are preparing for war by making weapons and conducting research into the most efficient means of causing destruction to humanity. Why make weapons if they are not to be used? History abounds in examples that weapons that have been amassed have ended up being used; in this century, nuclear weapons have been used.

It is estimated that some one hundred million people, who could more profitably be engaged in tasks conducive to peace and harmony, are engaged in the fulfillment of military tasks. Some of the best brains, some five to six hundred thousand of the most highly qualified scientists and technicians, are applying their energies, intelligence, and skills to the invention, production, and improvement of weapons that could destroy millions and millions of people. The two leading powers, the United States and the Soviet Union, have between them a stockpile of some fifty thousand nuclear warheads with a destructive capacity of over 1.3 million times more than the bomb that was dropped on Hiroshima.[18]

On the one hand, the manufacture of these weapons is a measure of the high-level scientific advancement of our era; on the other, the cost involved, in the face of all the problems that beset humankind, is indeed senseless. For resources ploughed into weapons and weapons research contribute to poverty, poor health, illiteracy, infant mortality, unemployment, and other ills that afflict us. The cost of one new nuclear submarine, for instance, could provide the annual education budget of twenty-three developing countries with 160 million school-age children.[19]

But it is not only the big powers and other highly industrialized nations that are engaged in this senseless arms race. The poor nations, which can ill afford it, are often more involved in terms of per capita expenditure than the big powers, and this is where the tragic nature of the arms buildup becomes even clearer. Africa, according to the United States Center for Defense Information, is increasingly spending money on the acquisition of arms; military spending rose by over 400 percent from 3.8 billion in 1973 to $16.9 billion in 1983. During the same ten-year period, the percentage of their GNP that African countries spent on their armed forces rose from 2.7 percent to 4.5 percent. The biggest armies in Africa were those of Ethiopia (a country synonymous with hunger), Nigeria, Angola, Zaire, and Zimbabwe.

Africa's military imports have also been increasing at an alarming rate. This rise, according to the same report, was higher than that of other Third World regions, except the Middle East, which had a 43 percent increase. These imports included tanks and self-propelled guns (1,800), artillery pieces (4,400), armored carriers (3,800), naval craft (152), military aircraft (1,000), helicopters (361), and surface-to-air missiles (1,275). These cost a staggering amount of money, taking away much-needed resources that could have been used to address the very urgent problems that face Africa.

The tragedy is that while military spending is a major cause of Africa's poverty and underdevelopment (for every soldier in Africa, fifty children are deprived of education), the manufacturers of the military weapons are making huge profits from the African nations that purchase them. The challenge is to all humankind, rich nations and poor nations, to come to appreciate the fact that arms buildup and military spending are a threat to peace and that peace should be the basic, global, and universal aim for every human being everywhere on the face of the globe.

Threats to the Safety of the Earth

The treats to the safety of the earth constitute a grim menace to the survival of human life and need to be taken seriously by all Christians. It is important for the church to emphasize the "caretaker" role of humankind, for the earth belongs to God and is a gift to humankind. It is equally important to draw the attention of the people of the highly industrialized nations, in both East and West, to the serious moral question of the dangers that their scientific and technological advances pose for the rest of humankind. While their scientific and technological advances have immensely benefited humankind, there is no gainsaying that these advances have also created a serious threat to the safety of the earth, for example, the pollution of the atmosphere by nuclear testing, accidents like Chernobyl that affect millions of people beyond the scene of mishap, and the dumping of nuclear waste, which shows a careless and disdainful attitude toward people's lives elsewhere. There is need to recognize that the world does not belong to the technological giants alone and that their interest and safety do not take precedence over others. If only we could accept the principle that we dare not wish anything for anyone that we would be unwilling to accept for ourselves, then the injustices that abound in our world would be eliminated.

The recommendations of a joint consultation of the Church and Society Unit of the World Council of Churches and the National Council of Churches in the Philippines entitled "New Technology, Work and Environment," pointed out:

> While science and technology have produced many important discoveries and material goods, the benefits of these are currently overshadowed by consequences which seriously damage the well-being of large sections of the human community and of the natural environment.[20]

The recommendations, which were endorsed by the Central Committee of the World Council of Churches, went on to draw attention to the following potentially hazardous consequences and by-products of science and technology:

(a) the rapid destruction and depletion of natural resources to a catastrophic extent.

(b) the poisoning of oceans, seas and rivers, the atmosphere, soil and food resources by chemicals, heavy metals and radiation, especially that caused by nuclear testing.

(c) the physical and social risks accompanying increasing militarization on a global scale, including related risks caused by nuclear power.

The responsibility of the churches in this critical area was expressed with refreshing clarity and admirable depth of understanding by the joint consultation in the following words:

> Committed as it is to the promotion of the integrity and the wholeness of relationships in all parts of creation, the church must struggle to protect and nourish the well-being of all people, especially of all people who fall easy prey to unjust structures and forces which divide and destroy. It must therefore of necessity take the side of the victims of growth. It must struggle to preserve and nourish our physical environment, which both guarantees the continuation of human life and is of value in its own right.

Racism and Apartheid

Racism continues to wax strong in our world today, even in predominantly Christian countries, in spite of all the claims by Christians to the oneness of humankind in Christ. Many people continue to suffer humiliation and even persecution at the hands of Christians and others, on the basis of their skin color or national origin. And in the Republic of South Africa the apartheid system of racial superiority and racial separation has reached unmatched heights of barbarity, which is a stain on the conscience of humankind.

Whatever interpretation may be given to racism, there is no gainsaying that any system of thought and action that engenders prejudice against other members of the human family simply because of the way the Creator created them is an arrogant attempt to impugn the wisdom of God in creating the variety of colors among the peoples of the world. In other words, racism is one way of saying that God should have been wise enough to give all human beings the same color. If there is any attitude that betrays lack of respect for God, it is racism. For no human being decided to make himself or herself; what we are is based on the wisdom of the Creator. All human beings have equal dignity in the sight of God, and I believe it is not possible for God to decree good for one segment of humanity without offering it equally to all, since the spirit of God dwells in all members of the human family.

Racism on the part of Christians cuts at the very root of their claims to belief in God and the person of Jesus Christ. For to make some members of the human family question their very essence or even entertain doubts about their humanity as a result of persistent racism is to make them question the goodness of their creation. The perpetrators of this evil are probably unaware that they are in open rebellion against God; sometimes they even invest their demonic practices with divine sanction based on spurious biblical interpretation.

Racism creates false divisions among humankind and leads to oppression and the violation of others' sense of being human. In its diabolical forms such as Nazism and apartheid, it leads to unbridgeable cleavages in the human community, and even to genocide.

But it is not only the victims of racism who suffer; the perpetrators also suffer, for it does incalculable violence to their humanity. An Akan maxim has it: "*Onipa gye nkannare a, osen dade*" (A rusty human being is worse than rusty iron). The perpetrators, of course, may not be aware of this debasement, since racial pride has blinded them and given them a false sense of their humanity; a false sense of power has given them a feeling of strength to determine who is human and who is not. But it is not within the power of any human group, however physically or politically powerful, to bestow humanity graciously on others. It is God's image in human beings that makes them human, and that image cannot be taken away by anybody.

The problem of apartheid in South Africa poses a serious challenge to humanity, from which no human being can escape responsibility. The church in particular must remain committed to the liberation of the children of God so that they can live as creatures of God. Beyers Naudé has said that the church

is where the people of God are, where life is being discovered again, the true meaning of love, of human community, of mutual concern for one another, of caring for people, of seeking true meaningful relationship, understanding not only between Christians but between all people.[21]

The world church cannot remain neutral in this situation; it must take the side of truth and unequivocally oppose apartheid as contrary to the will of God and Christian values. The solution to the problem of apartheid will lead to the creation of a just and healthy human community not only in South Africa but also in the whole world.

The methods for the dismantling of apartheid, of course, differ widely. Many Christians have taken the option of giving advice to the afflicted and debating whether violence is a Christian option. As Emilio Castro has said: "Those from outside must recall, when speaking about violence or non-violence, that it is not they, but others, who will be called upon to pay the price of following their advice."[22]

For fifty years the African National Congress used nonviolence as its weapon, but it met only with repeated acts of violent repression, as at Sharpeville. Now it has reversed its approach. When asked if he would fight Hitler with nonviolence, Gandhi, the apostle of nonviolence, said he would use violence against Hitler. So too the ANC has resorted to violence against the state violence of apartheid, which remains solidly entrenched. But those involved in the actual struggle are the persons to select their options; those outside need to exercise caution in passing judgment from a safe distance.

Of course, the victims of apartheid cannot go it alone; they need the support of others who will not compromise when the dignity of other children of God is brutally and severely assaulted with impunity. There are Christians in South Africa as well as outside who still feel committed to a nonviolent approach to the problem and have called for a national convention at which all the legitimate representatives and leaders of the people would sit and discuss the fate of South Africa. In recent years, there has been a call for sanctions, which has received varying degrees of support. These nonviolent approaches need the active support of Christians who are anxious to avoid a blood-bath and are willing to assume increasing responsibility in applying their collective pressure to remove the structures that keep the system of apartheid functioning. The need for the churches in the ecumenical movement to apply pressure on their governments and financial institutions to support nonviolent solutions to the problem cannot be overemphasized.

At this point, we need to take seriously Allan Boesak's call:

> Our call [to the people of Japan] is clear: we are asking for solidarity, we want you to help us by putting pressure on your government and the business community to stop collaborating with the Pretoria regime against us; and do not be misled by the South African government's statement that it is reforming the system. Apartheid cannot be reformed. The best remedy for it is immediate change for a democratically elected government involving all South Africans. And do not also be misled by the argument propagated by the friends of the Pretoria regime that sanctions will harm the Africans. What you ought to know is that argument is not in our interest but rather in the interest of the very people who purportedly are sympathizing with us. We are now imbued with the preternatural instinct to know that the immediate concern of those who propagate that line of thought is profit.[23]

Our partisan interests do not permit us to acknowledge the threats to peace and security in our world today; this leads to giving aid and comfort to oppressors and helping to perpetuate the conditions for war. But it needs to be appreciated that racism and oppression are threats to peace in our world. For the apartheid system can engulf the whole world in a bloody confrontation if steps are not taken to eliminate it, and it is not only the victims of apartheid who should regard racism as a threat to peace.

The availability of nuclear weapons and the threat they pose to the safety of all humankind have led many people to associate peace with nuclear disarmament. The facts regarding a nuclear war are indeed frightening. A 1983 World Health Organization study stated that in a nuclear war one billion people would be killed outright in the first exchange of nuclear weapons, and an additional billion people would die from injuries, blast, fire, and radiation. Christians and all people of goodwill must relentlessly seek ways and means of achieving nuclear disarmament in order to secure peace and security for the entire world.

But even if all the nuclear arsenals were destroyed and a complete and absolute halt were put to the manufacture of nuclear weapons, as well as other weapons, the oppression resulting from racism would remain.

SEARCH FOR GOD'S INTENTION FOR US TODAY

In the face of these persistent factors that militate against the achievement of community and a harmonious and peaceful world, Christians must relentlessly try to discern God's intention for us in our world today. This search must be based on the firm conviction that in the end God's will shall reign supreme.

The resources of the Christian faith do not bestow boundless privileges on Christians; understood in their proper context, they define the role Christians are called upon to play in the face of the challenges that confront the world. Our responses should lead toward increasing the full meaning of the Christian symbol of the cross, which, significantly, stood between two other crosses, showing God's close relationship with humankind. And as God has been united with us so must Christians work to overcome the structures that support a divided world, for God does not divide humankind. Metropolitan Mar Osthathios said at the Commission on Faith and Order meeting in Bangalore in 1978:

> The unity of humanity is to be modeled on trinitarian unity.... Ultimately all differences and separations between human beings have to be dissolved in a mutual *perichoresis* (embracing, penetrating, not merely sharing) where "thine and mine" are not different in case of property, purpose and will but different only in different

personal and group identities with full openness to and penetration of each other.... The mystery of the unity of humanity in Christ, patterned on the mystery of the triune unity of the Godhead, has high significance for our social goals also.... Ultimately, parochialism, insularity, division, separation, class, ethnic conflict, political and economic injustice, exploitation and oppression have to be judged by this criterion.[24]

The resources of the African tradition have an important bearing on the pursuit of community. The sense of community (though it may not always be put into practice), the emphasis on relationship as the basis of humanity,[25] the emphasis on cooperation and mutual helpfulness, the notion of humankind as caretaker with respect to nature are all worth seriously considering in our search. The symbol of the Siamese crocodile provides a motif for understanding the relationship that exists between all peoples. The heads represent diversity, not division, but the common stomach clearly shows what the heads have in common, which in fact sustains them; our interests are not divergent but convergent. In the relationship between the North and the South, the Brandt Commission report said: "The South cannot grow adequately without the North. The North cannot prosper or improve its situation unless there is greater progress in the South."[26] The mutual advantage that cooperation can bring about accrues to all and not to a segment of humankind.

In the disparity in wealth between North and South there is furthermore a crucial issue of morality at stake. For the poverty of the South is not entirely of the South's own making; the North has some responsibility for it since its development was made possible by the labor and resources of the South. There is a moral necessity to recognize this and to act accordingly. But the solution of the problem, the bridging of the gap, does not rest with the North alone; the South has to make great efforts and persevere, to defend its legitimate rights or forfeit them.

John Pobee points out the responsibility of those who wield power by citing the Akan proverb that genuine persons of power do not ruin the state of which they are head; rather they are responsible for seeing to the welfare and peace of the people.[27] The self-respect of the powerful is forfeited if they ruin the state by using their power and influence to make others poor. On the other hand, their self-respect is maintained if they use their power to help the people. But those who do not have power have their share of responsibility. As the Akan proverb puts it, *"Woankasa a, wode wo sekan gua onanka"* (If you remain silent, others will skin a snake with your knife) — which is one way of saying that those who do not have power must defend their rights or forfeit them.

If the church devotes attention to the arena where the social and political imperatives of our day impinge forcefully on us, then it will be bringing the message of the gospel to bear on our total lives; it will be acting out the life of our Savior, whose life was broken for all humankind. In endeavoring to eliminate the forces that militate against the achievement of community and the unity of humankind, we can be guided by another African proverb: "When spider webs unite they can tie up a lion."

Notes

1. See *West Africa*, no. 3666 (November 16, 1987): 2258.

2. See *North-South: A Program for Survival — The Report of the Independent Commission on International Development Issues*, under the chairmanship of Willy Brandt (London, 1980), 32.

3. *Guidelines on Dialogue with People of Living Faiths and Ideologies* (Geneva: WCC, 1979), 34.

4. See Mercy Oduyoye, *Hearing and Knowing: Theological Reflections on Christianity in Africa* (Maryknoll, N.Y.: Orbis Books, 1986), 116.

5. Ibid., 119.

6. Masao Takenaka, *God Is Rice: Asian Culture and Christian Faith* (Geneva: WCC Publications, 1986), 24.

7. John Pobee, "Who Are the Poor?" in *The Beatitudes as a Call to Community* (Geneva: WCC Publications, 1987), 60.

8. E. Obiechina, *Culture, Tradition and Society in the East African Novel* (Cambridge, 1975), 42.

9. *Religious Experience in Humanity's Relation with Nature: A Consultation* (Yaounde, Cameroon/Geneva: WCC Publications, 1978), 14.

10. *Decolonizing the Mind: The Politics of Language in African Literature* (London: James Currey, 1986), 3.

11. *Proceedings of the First International Congress of Africanists, Accra, 1962* (London, Oxford University Press), 50, 51.

12. Takenaka, *God Is Rice*, 37.

13. See *West Africa*, no. 3663 (October 26, 1982): 2125.

14. Pobee, "Who Are the Poor?" in *The Beatitudes*, 62.

15. Harold Lever and Christopher Huhne, *Debt and Danger: The World Financial Crisis* (New York: Atlanta Monthly, 1985), 141.

16. See *Development Forum* (published by the UN Division for Economic and Social Information/DPI and the United Nations University) 15, no. 3 (April 1982): 1, 10, 11.

17. Ibid.

18. See Marian Dobrosielski, "The 'Cost' of Today's Peace," in *Work in Progress* (United Nations University) 10, no. 3 (October 1987): 3.

19. Ibid.

20. "The World around Us: Its Integrity and Ours," in *Church and Society Newsletter*, no. 6 (May 1987): 3.

21. Beyers Naudé and Dorothee Sölle, *Hope for Faith: A Conversation* (Geneva: WCC Publications/Grand Rapids: William B. Eerdmans, 1986), 21.

22. *Letter from the General Secretary of the WCC*, September 1987.

23. *West Africa*, no. 3669 (December 7, 1987): 2386.

24. As quoted by Oduyoye, *Hearing and Knowing*, 142.

25. Ibid., 141.

26. Pobee, "Who Are the Poor?" in *The Beatitudes*, 33.

27. Ibid., 61.

2

TOWARD A HOLISTIC VIEW
OF SALVATION

Kofi Asare Opoku

Salvation is one of the key concepts in Christianity, and
for most people it is the core of the Christian faith. In the
different traditions within Christendom, salvation is given
various interpretations. In the Roman Catholic and Eastern
Orthodox churches, salvation is basically regarded as the
"deification of the man by participation in supernatural
grace," since the destiny of human beings is participation in divine life. In the Protestant tradition, salvation
is essentially the "restoration of a broken personal relationship" between God and humankind. The relationship
was broken as a result of humankind's sin against God,
and salvation is, in this sense, the result of the forgiveness
of sins.[1] The overwhelming thrust of the meaning given
to salvation by Christian missionaries in mission fields,
which was received by many converts to the Christian
faith, was that of salvation of the soul from sin, which is
understood to be essentially a revolt against God, human
beings setting themselves up in place of God.

According to the teaching of the church, the restoration
of the broken relationship between God and humankind
was effected in the person of Jesus Christ, who is the only
mediator between God and human beings. It followed,
therefore, that only those who believed in Jesus Christ and
accepted him as Savior and Lord would benefit from his
work of atoning for the sins of humankind. Those who
did not accept Jesus Christ, those who were outside the
church, had no claim to God's free offer through Jesus

Christ, and, in fact, there was no salvation outside the church.

From the point of view of the church's own history, which glorified its exclusive claim to the right knowledge about God and truth about God, this position was only a continuation of the history of the church's self-understanding. For the church understood itself as having received a special mission in the Great Commission (Matt. 28:18–20), to make disciples of all people, and it could therefore not undercut its own divinely given self-image and mission by proclaiming a message that would jeopardize the position of Jesus Christ as God's final self-revelation. God's saving activity was only through Christ, and it was a logical consequence of this affirmation to endeavor to convert all people outside the church into the fold of the community that was saved. For in this community the ultimate meaning of human existence was believed to be found.

It hardly needs stressing that such a view of ultimate reality necessitated the rejection and downgrading of other views that differed from it. It was therefore no wonder that other religions came to be regarded as the work of the devil, and those who practiced other faiths were seen as the enemies of God who deserved to be defeated by those who had been bestowed with divine privilege.

But this position clearly ignores the possibility of human error in the appropriation of divine revelation. A degree of finality is attached to human understanding that is out of step with human finiteness.[2] At the same time, the freedom of God is denied, for God's thoughts have to coincide with human thought and understanding. Besides, to limit salvation to members of the church is to limit severely the arena of God's activity; it is to limit the freedom of God to act outside the confines of the church. In short, it amounts to tying God to one place.

Seen from the perspective of the people who were targets of missionary evangelization, a strong element in the missionary thrust was the close identification of Christianity with the self-image of the West. The West saw itself as inheritors of Christianity, which it considered its own.

It was their personal possession that they were bringing to others who were outside their own linear salvation history and who had to be brought in to achieve significance. Georges Khodr has written:

> The history of the Christian church becomes history itself. What occurs in the experience of the west fashions history. The rest of the world remains ahistorical until it adopts western experience which, moreover, by implacable logic and technological determinism, is destined to dominate the world. This philosophy of history will in its turn leave its stamp on theological thought, its basic outlook and methods. Thus the religion of the under-developed countries which have not apparently been influenced by the dynamics of creative civilization ... being still a historically inferior era, will have to pass into a superior stage, to be historicized by adopting the superior hierarchical type of Christianity. The rest of the world must come into the time continuum of the church through a salvation achieved by the extension of the Christian way of life founded on the authority of the west.[3]

The idea of a linear salvation history in which God acts smacks of divine favoritism. For in practical terms, it is the divinely favored ones who are within the orbit of salvation history and the less favored ones are to be brought in. This may imply further that God is absent in the history of other peoples, and this amounts to a denial of God's providence and power. In fact, it was largely due to the assumption that God had not acted in the history of others that the conviction became firmly buttressed that those who possess the truth are those in whose history God has acted. Such an attitude tended to engender feelings of disrespect or condescension toward others, while at the same time it closed the mind to the possibility that others may have something to give or share concerning the relations between God and humankind.

But increasingly many Christians, in the ecumenical movement as well as among Roman Catholics, have come to revise their seemingly unbending position about salvation and to admit that there is the possibility of salvation outside the church. Vatican II declared:

> those also can attain to everlasting salvation who through
> no fault of their own do not know Christ or His church,
> yet sincerely seek God and, moved by grace, strive by
> their deeds to do His will as it is known to them through
> the dictates of conscience.[4]

While this statement represents a refreshing shift from the
inflexible position of the past concerning those who can
be saved, it is instructive to note that the power of pro-
nouncement, in the past as well as in the present, still
seems to reside in the church. It was the church that at
one time said those who were outside it had no possibility
of being saved; now the same church is saying that after
all there is a possibility for outsiders, and this shows it
has realized its own error.

But this raises the question as to what experience in
other religions may be compared to the salvation to which
Christians tend to lay exclusive claim. We cannot, however, do justice to this question without first widening
our understanding of God and breaking loose from the
restricted understanding that has taken centuries to crys-
tallize and that persists to this day. God is the God of all
humankind and God is not so unkind as to have refused
to be disclosed to some peoples. God's divine truth and
salvation have not been confined to a few favored people;
on the contrary, God is God because God is accessible to
all, and even though we may have different experiences
of God through our appropriation of God's self-disclosure,
we do well remember that this is not the whole of God's
self-disclosure, for God is greater than our understanding
of God. Commenting on Christianity's tendency to deny
God's involvement and salvific activity in other religions,
including African traditional religion, Maimela has written:

> for to deny God's saving activity in other religions will
> be to confuse our Christian ideas about God with God's
> reality itself which transcends all finite, human images
> that we as humans may ever hope to construct in order to
> portray God's presence among us. It is as we realize that
> God is greater than any religious system and its thought-
> patterns that we will be in a position to listen and study

sympathetically how God's salvific activity is experienced and understood in African Traditional Religion.[5]

The deep experience of Christians with God is described as salvation through Christ's death on the cross, which atoned for the sins of human beings and rescued them from eternal damnation, which is the consequence of sin. To Christians, this is the ultimate action of God toward sinful humankind. The experiences of people in other religions of God's dealings with them may be described as an experience of deliverance from life-threatening situations, liberation from oppressors, or rescue from any danger that threatens life. In other words, the saving acts of God as people experience them may not be restricted to salvation or deliverance from sin and guilt and redemption through Christ's death on the cross; rather they may cover a wide range of problems that people perceive to be real and fundamental to the human condition and that they need God's saving power to overcome. The result of this divine activity is freedom from threats to life, unity with God, divine favor, abundant life, well-being, and blessedness.

It is clear therefore that the experience of being saved, delivered, rescued, or liberated varies with people's conceptions of what constitute basic and fundamental problems in the human situation. From these varying conceptions there arise equally varying remedies or antidotes to what is perceived to be the problem. But we cannot make one conception the yardstick by which other conceptions are measured, as the tendency has often been for Christians to make their own understanding of salvation from individual sin and guilt through Christ's death on the cross the basic perspective from which to view other perspectives — usually found wanting.

The crux of the matter is that people are saved, liberated, delivered, or rescued from what is real to them in their authentic and existential condition, and that answers to questions that people have not asked, regardless of how "universal" we may regard them to be, are never *real answers*. It is as we listen to how others understand the human problem and how it is to be solved that we can deepen our understanding of ourselves as members of the human family and increase our knowledge of the many ways in which people experience God's dealings with them. And if we start from the clear and unequivocal conviction that God is present with all peoples and is involved in their lives, then we can affirm that God has not been absent from all their serious efforts to make sense of their own life and destiny.

THE BIBLE AND SALVATION

The Bible speaks of salvation in a variety of ways. In the Old Testament, the Exodus story recounts the most important single event of salvation. God saved the Israelites from the shackles of Egyptian domination and this event became the creed, as Von Rad called it.[6] This event became the point of reference and provided the basis for the covenant upon which the Decalogue and its subsequent elaboration were based.[7] The Exodus was a concrete historical event but it also became the basis for faith in God and what God would do in the future. There is therefore a spiritual dimension to this particular event of salvation from physical bondage.

In the story of the bronze serpent (Num. 21), we find another vivid example of God's saving acts in the experience of the Israelites. When they complained against Moses and God after leaving Mount Hor and heading for the vicinity of Edom, a fiery serpent bit many of them to death. And when the people repented for what they had done, God provided a bronze serpent; all those bitten, if they looked upon the bronze serpent, were healed. This was a salvation in physical terms of recovering from the snake bite, but at the same time it was also salvation from spiritual sickness. It took faith to look up to the bronze serpent on the pole; this required of the victims of the snake bite both repentance and trust in God. The healing of the victims involved an act of faith.

In the New Testament we also find a variety of ways of understanding salvation. The evidence that the reign of

God is at hand (Mark 1:15) is that the blind receive their
sight, the lame walk, lepers are cleansed, the deaf hear,
the dead are raised, the poor have good news preached
to them (Luke 7:18–23). In his sermon at Nazareth (Luke
4:16–21), Jesus speaks of salvation in terms of liberty to
the captives, the recovery of sight to the blind, and the
freeing of the oppressed. In Acts 16:29–32, Paul and Silas
respond to the jailer's question of what he should do to be
saved by inviting him to believe in the Lord Jesus Christ.

St. Paul speaks of a bodily resurrection (1 Cor. 15) to
show that salvation is not only spiritual but also physical;
and in Romans 8:18–24, 38–39, Paul also gives a cosmic
dimension to salvation when he says that "the creation
waits with eager longing for the revealing of the children
of God" and "the creation itself will be set free from its
bondage to decay and obtain the glorious liberty of the
children of God." Paul related the longing of the individual
to become a child of God with the groaning of the whole
creation to be set free from its bondage. Here individual
salvation is linked to the redemption of the whole created
order.[8]

Christians have never read the Bible from a neutral
standpoint, and quite often the reader's own interests and
background influence his or her interpretation. This has
led to a variety of ways of understanding the idea of salvation and the various emphases that are given to it by
groups of Christians. Salvation means for some the forgiveness of sins or the entry into heaven after death, a
notion that limits the biblical understanding, while others
insist that salvation has to do with the establishment of
God's reign of justice, righteousness, and peace here on
earth.

The biblical evidence does not support any one-sided
interpretation of salvation, which Christians have often
given. The whole person, not just the soul, is involved
in salvation. Mbiti has written:

> What is important here is to consider biblical salvation
> in holistic terms. Man is the object of God's salvation as
> it is narrated and recorded in the Bible. And man is both

physical and spiritual. So biblical salvation embraces those entities together. When only one is stressed at the expense of the other, a distortion of biblical salvation ensues and one part of man is virtually excluded and starved out.[9]

SALVATION IN THE AFRICAN EXPERIENCE

Patrick Kalilombe has written:

> The African Bible reader will thus not fear to state that the religious systems of his ancestors were not just tolerated by God. They were the results of the efforts of our cultures wherein the spirit of God was an active agent. And therefore, there would be no fear in me to assert that, as long as these religions were the serious searchings of our cultures for the deity, they are to be respected as the normal divinely given means of salvation, put by God in his will for the salvation of all the peoples.[10]

This view of the African traditional religious heritage as the result of God's action to save God's own children does not mean that there are no blemishes in it in the sight of God and that every aspect of it must be upheld and perpetuated. All human efforts at understanding the activity of God and God's self-disclosure are partial, limited, and subject to error and sin. What is being suggested here is that the good elements inherent in this particular religious heritage were put there by God; this points out clearly that God has no favorites and does not hide divine truth from some and disclose it only to other favored ones. In the active presence of God with all God's people, we find good and valid elements that come out of that divine presence.

The acceptance of the idea that God shares divine truth with all and that the experience of God's grace, love, and saving power is not unique to Christians can save us from the temptation to assume a position of superiority as possessors of the only truth and therefore to despise, reject, or condemn others and cause further divisions among member's of the human family.

Although God has not withheld divine truth from people, we must admit that there are different ways of understanding this truth, as well as different ways of expressing what is wrong with the human condition and how that problem is to be solved.

In the traditional African setting to which Christianity came, the experience of being saved or rescued from danger so that one could continue to live was quite common. Brief attention to words used in one of the African languages, Akan, to describe this experience can help shed light on this experience. These same words were used in the translation of the Bible to convey the Christian concept of salvation, and although Christian evangelists, preachers, and converts used these words, their cultural as well as social background was often not fully appreciated.

To save someone from danger or any life-threatening situation or to rescue someone from perishing, in the experience of the Akan is *gye no nkwa* (to save his or her life). *Gye* means "save" or "rescue," and *nkwa* is "life." The noun *agyenkwa* (savior, rescuer) means the one who performs the saving act, who takes the endangered person to safety or prevents whatever may have threatened to take that person's life. The act of saving or rescuing is *nkwagye*, and it can refer either to rescue from physical dangers — wild animals, poisonous snakes, fire, floods, disease — or spiritual dangers — attacks by witches, sorcerers, or other demonic forces that threaten life. Medicine men, priests, and priestesses were and still are the professional people who are equipped by their training to deal with such cases.

A related term, which comes from the experience of war to defend our societies from attack by hostile people, is that of *osagyefo*. This title refers to the one who saves in battle, the redeemer, or the one who wins a war to save his people from being decimated by their enemies or taken into slavery. This title was applied to some of the Akan kings, such as the king of the Asante nation. There is also the title of *osabarima*, the great warrior who leads the people to victory against their enemies. These titles are still in use by Akan kings and chiefs who have inherited the stools of great warriors of the past; they are a constant reminder of the great achievements of the past and serve as a source of inspiration for present-day rulers.

In traditional life, people turned to God as the final source of rescue, especially when all human efforts failed. In this sense, God was their Savior who saved them from extreme life-threatening situations such as serious illness, floods, pestilence, famine, drought, and war. It is quite common among the Akan for a herbalist to say to a patient: *"Se Onyame ma kwan a, metumi asa wo yare"* (If God permits, I shall be able to cure you). Ultimately God is the source of the healing process, and God heals when people fall ill. God is also said to be the determiner of destiny, and if God does not decree your death you do not die: *Onyame ankum wo a, wunwu.*

In time of extreme danger, people shout, *"Agya ei!,"* a call to God to come to the rescue. And those who survive a life-threatening experience are wont to say, *"Se ennye Onyame a..."* (Had it not been for God...) or, *"Onyame adaworoma"* (It was by God's grace).

Some of the Akan names for God also show how the people conceive of God. God is *Amosu* (Giver of water) and *Totrobonsu* (the One who causes rain to fall copiously); thus God saves human beings and nature from the draught that could kill all living things. God is *Awowia* (Giver of sunshine, which sustains life on earth). God is *Abommubuwafre* (Consoler or Comforter who gives salvation), *Amoamee* (Giver of sufficiency or satisfaction), and *Nyaamanekose* (One in whom we confide the troubles that come upon us). All these names show how God is understood to be related to God's children.

Similar notions of God are found in other parts of the continent. A Galla prayer from Ethiopia and Kenya says:

> O God, it is in peace that I have rested,
> Make me walk straight on this road [that is, safely],
> If I speak, take calumny from my lips,
> If I hunger, take away my pride,
> May I pass this day in calling upon you,
> O Master that knows no other master.[11]

The Barundi call God *Rutangaboro* (the Protector of the poor) and *Ntirandekuva* (the One who has not let me drop yet), which means that God is the protector of life. To the Illa of Zambia, God is *Luvhunabaumba* (Deliverer of those in trouble).

Proverbs are another expression of the experience of God among people in traditional Africa. The Akan say, "If God gives you a calabash of palm-wine and an evil-minded person kicks it over, God fills it up for you again," meaning that God's providence is unfailing. They also say, "If God gives you sickness, God also gives you the cure." The Burundi say, "A tree protected by God cannot be hurt by the wind," which expresses the idea that people are safe in God's hands. And when the Illa of Zambia say that "God has long arms," they are referring to the care, protection, and security that they experience from God.

God, however, is not the only focus of appeal in traditional Africa. The ancestors and divinities are also prayed to for help in time of trouble, but it is always understood that the ultimate power comes from God.

All the saving acts that people experience are acts that contribute to the protection of life here on earth, abundance of life, good health, and prosperity. Mbiti has written:

> In these religious considerations of the concept of *salvation*, we take note that salvation in African religion has to do with physical and immediate dangers (of the individual and more often of the community) — dangers that threaten individual or community survival, good health and general prosperity or safety. This is the main religious setting in which the notion of salvation is understood and experienced. Salvation is not just an abstraction, it is concrete, told in terms of both what has happened and is likely to be encountered by people as they go through daily experiences.[12]

The dangers that people face are not only physical but also spiritual. Moreover, the people who experience salvation or deliverance from these dangers are all creatures of God who have bodies that are material and subject to the destructive forces of death and decay, as well as spirits that are immaterial and sparks of the divine that link human beings directly to the Creator. A human being is a combination of these two elements and this notion of human personality is basic to the understanding of the human predicament as it is understood in the African religious heritage. The human predicament has aspects that are material and aspects that are spiritual, and both are held in perspective. One aspect does not overshadow the other in the understanding of the human condition. Since the unity of human personality is a fundamental assumption in traditional African thought and the human being is not a divided entity, a clear-cut distinction is not made between the material and the spiritual as if they were separate entities. The Akan perform a soul-cleansing ritual, *akraguare*, in which a person who has been defiled takes a ritual bath. The person bathes the body with water in which some leaves with cleansing properties are put, but he or she is at the same time bathing or cleansing the soul.

An important question that relates to salvation in the traditional African experience is whether salvation has to do with the moral life of the individual or that of the community. Certainly the traditional community has its notions of right and wrong, and there is a general understanding that what is wrong goes against human life and so is also directed against the Creator who created every person and upon whom all things depend.[13]

Maimela has commented that sin is interpreted as lack of love in communal relationships more than

> in terms of a divine retributive law which must be obeyed and whose justice must be satisfied by human beings in their relationship with God. For, in the final analysis, it is not the self-sufficient God who suffers or benefits from human activity but our fellow humans who are impoverished or enriched by what we do to them.[14]

A Mende myth from Sierra Leone, which explains why the Mende call God *Leve* (the One who is up or high), says in part:

From the place where He stayed, He made two things, one for the man and one for the woman, which He named fowl. When He handed them over, He said, "Whenever one of you does wrong to his companion you must call Me, and when I come you must give Me back my fowl!" They agreed. He then returned to His own town. When anyone did wrong to his companion he always said, "*Ngewo yei — O' ngi bi le ve* (O God, come down, I wish to give you your fowl); this imprecation has now become a signal for a curse. Whenever a person who does wrong hears these words uttered, he will apologize at once, instead of allowing God to come down for the fowl to kill it. One day, *Ngewo* came down to them and said "Farewell." He then exhorted them saying, "See, I have made an agreement with you, concerning your dealing with one another; therefore do not have a bad heart (bear malice) toward one another." They replied, "Yes." Then He went up to His place. From that time they called Him *Leve* (Up, High).[15]

What we do to each other also involves God, as this myth clearly shows.

Christianity introduced a new concept of salvation through the cross of Christ and tended to emphasize salvation from sin and guilt and eternal damnation. The missionary church also denied the existence of witches, demons, and evil forces, a reality to most African people, without realizing that it was merely being Western but not necessarily biblical. For the Bible acknowledges the existence of principalities and powers and the rulers of darkness in this world, as well as demons, but it teaches that God's power overcomes them all. For the hearers of missionary preaching, Christ could not be Savior unless he also addressed himself to the preoccupations of the people with their mundane problems of witchcraft, demons, and evil forces, as well as with infertility, failure, and other problems of daily life.

In the missionary churches, this emphasis on salvation from sin and guilt and the denial of the existence of evil forces created a barrier between the pastor and the parishioners. The average parishioners could not bare their problems to the pastor, whereas the same parishioners would not hesitate to bare their problems to a priest at a shrine.

The rise of the indigenous churches, also called independent churches — to which people take all their problems, fears, and anxieties about demons, witches, and sorcerers as well as problems of lack of success, ill health, infertility, and other misfortunes — indicates clearly that there is continuity between these new churches and the traditional religion that helped people to cope successfully with problems of daily life. These indigenous churches have given us a wider understanding of salvation in the Christian context as they provide meaningful relief or deliverance from problems of daily life and are not only concerned with sin and the hereafter.

As Mbiti has written: "Thus African peoples find salvation to be meaningful in areas far beyond the limitations of evangelical theology which has more or less confined the term to the question of sin."[16]

There cannot be one prescribed understanding of what salvation should be, based on the easy assumption that what Christians regard to be problems and questions should be the same for others as well. Instead, we need to listen to the problems and questions that others raise in their context in order to understand the human condition in its totality and God's dealing with humankind in its widest perspective.

In the African context, there is the need for salvation in other areas of our lives that have hitherto not been given requisite attention in discussions of the meaning and implications of salvation. There are many areas in our lives where deliverance from oppression is sorely needed. As a result of the combined colonial and missionary enterprise, there occurred a despising and debasement of Africans based on a disdainful attitude toward traditional religion and culture and a wholesale condemnation of African ways of life. This resulted in a deeply wounded African spirit. There is a need for restoration and wholeness so that Africans may see in their Africanness an individualized expression of God, the Creator, and contribute to other members of the human family the gifts that God bestowed on God's African children. At the same time those who hold negative views about Africans need to be delivered from their bondage.

Although we must affirm the good in the African cultural heritage, there remain other areas of the culture that are oppressive. The fear of witchcraft and demonic forces, for example, hold many Africans in bondage and call for liberation so that people will be free to live wholesome lives.

There is also a need for salvation from the dependency syndrome that has become a feature of contemporary Africa. The dependence of African Christians on European theology and church structures and the imitation that continues to characterize much of Christian life in Africa takes away much originality and resourcefulness. In the effort to come to a broader understanding of salvation in Africa today, there is a need to encourage people to stand on their own feet and maintain their dignity as human beings and not to be put at the receiving end all the time. This need for self-reliance also applies to the socio-economic aspects of life in Africa.

Meaningful salvation cannot ignore the harsh problems of racism, political oppression, neocolonialism, and economic exploitation for which many Africans feel the urgent need for liberation. The church needs to address itself to all these problems in order to make the salvation that Christ brings relevant to every aspect of our lives.

SALVATION IN A GLOBAL CONTEXT

Christians have often taken refuge in the salvation of the soul and concentrated on "spiritual" matters and individual salvation and paid less attention to the whole person. This dualistic notion is certainly not biblical, but rather shows the influence of Greek philosophy. Jae Shik Oh has commented:

> There is...the latent attitude in the Christian community that the spirit is more valuable than the body, and that

the body may be shared for the sake of the spirit. As a corollary, Christians protect their spiritual territory jealously but are less concerned about the destruction of the body. They fight hard to protect the sanctuary but are careless about what is happening in torture chambers. This attitude has profound social implications. [It assumes] that earthly matters can be sacrificed for the sake of heavenly concerns. Hence Christians are more concerned with authority and order in a society, but careless about the destruction of the earth. The groaning of the earth and the cries from the torture chamber have not reached Christian ears.[17]

The preference of the spiritual to the material, the soul to the body, has often led Christians to close their eyes to human suffering. This has often given the false impression that mundane matters do not receive God's attention. It is what may be described as the "Northern Captivity" of the church, from which Christian theology needs to be liberated. There are still many Christians who think that there is only one way of doing theology and have not as yet appropriated their spiritual heritage as an important ingredient for the doing of theology in their lands. And yet this is an important task that will help liberate the theological captors from the grip of their own distortions.

The Exodus story has inspired hope in many Christians in Africa and other areas of the South to address themselves to the socio-political conditions in the contemporary world. When people read Exodus 3:7ff. — "I have seen the affliction of my people who are in Egypt, and have heard their cry because of their taskmasters; I know their sufferings, and I have come down to deliver them out of the hand of the Egyptians" — they know that God will come to deliver them because God hears the cry of the afflicted and oppressed peoples and has real concern with life on earth.

Salvation cannot be wholly understood without its socio-political dimension, and there is still the need to free the captives from the political and economic pharaohs of this world.[18] This effort is clearly buttressed by the prophetic call for justice found in the Bible:

Shame on the man who builds his house by non-justice and completes its upstairs rooms by non-right, who makes his fellow man work for nothing, without paying him his wages, who says, "I will build myself an imposing palace with spacious rooms upstairs," who sets windows in it, panels it with cedar, and paints it vermilion. (Jer. 22:13–14)

The demand for justice by those to whom it is denied economically, politically, and socially in our world today must be seen as part of their salvation that is yet to be unfolded. And as the cry for justice continues, the pharaohs are also being given the opportunity to be freed from their own positions of bondage in order to conform to the will of God:

The kind of fasting I want is this: Remove the chains of oppression and the yoke of injustice, and let the oppressed go free. Share your food with the hungry and open your homes to the homeless poor. Give clothes to those who have nothing to wear, and do not refuse to help your own relatives. (Isa. 58:6–7)

There is no self-righteousness here, for what is at stake is the will of God as the prophets made it known not only in their time but also in our own. It is meant to free both captors and captives.

The oppressors need to be freed by those whom they oppress from their own tragic concepts in which they are imprisoned. In the South African situation, for example, the oppressed people are showing the oppressors that the oppressed are the ones who are strong. Beyers Naudé posed the question to blacks, "But don't you hate us whites for what you have experienced in pain and suffering?" And the answer came:

In the beginning I feared, and then I hated, and then I discovered, no, I am the one who is strong, because I have to pity this person. He is a victim, he is imprisoned in his own tragic concept, and therefore he is unfree and I am free.[19]

And Naudé concluded that once you hear that from a person who has been severely tortured and you catch something of the tremendous warmth of that spirit of love and community and of forgiveness, then you begin to understand that there is a totally new perspective to the Christian faith, which these people in certain situations of crisis convey to you.

There is need to deepen our understanding of sin, as some of the World Council of Churches' proclamations are already pointing out; then our understanding of salvation will equally be deepened and broadened. The planning for destruction that is so much a part of our technological age, the destruction of the environment, the meaningless research to perfect the weapons of destruction instead of to benefit humankind and improve the quality of life, are all signs of the clutches of the technological monster from which we need to be freed. Dorothee Sölle has said:

> If you say truly it is a sin against the Creator, the Redeemer and the Spirit to build and test nuclear weapons, that is a very clear statement of faith, and not just a statement of reason. And if you say you cannot feed the poor with bombs, you need something else for them, it is a similar statement which is very clear.... I am thinking about the community of scientists and engineers, which is an important group of people, who need that conversion out of their purposeless and meaningless doing of research.[20]

God saves us in the totality of our human existence. In this holistic view of salvation, the seeming lack of concern of God with human problems — which comes from an exclusive understanding of salvation as deliverance from sin and guilt — gives way to a view of God as the One who has real concern with human life on earth, the One who out of great compassion saves us from all that oppresses us. Mercy Oduyoye has written:

> In the pastoral letter to Titus (3:5) we find a doctrine on which we are called to rely. In God's compassion he saves those who are misled and enslaved by passions and luxuries, those who live in wickedness and ill-will, those

who hate each other and are hateful themselves, by the water of rebirth and renewal in the Holy Spirit.... All nations, all Christians have to live in the knowledge of what Deuteronomy puts before Israel. A people saved by God have the Kingdom of God as their priority; and this is the purpose for which Jesus lived and died. Liberated from the principalities and powers of this realm we continue to work and live before God. That is salvation.[21]

Biblical teaching on salvation needs to be investigated today more thoroughly than ever before. Its lessons will aid our efforts at building community in our broken and divided world.

Notes

1. See Van A. Harvey, *A Handbook of Theological Terms* (New York: Macmillan, 1964), 225.

2. Kofi Asare Opoku, "Issues in Dialogue between African Traditional Religion and Christianity," in *Towards A Dialogue between Christians and Traditionalists in Africa*, report of a consultation held at Mindolo Ecumenical Foundation, Kitwe, September 22–25, 1986 (Geneva, World Council of Churches), 4–9.

3. "The Economy of the Spirit," in *Mission Trends No. 5: Faith Meets Faith*, Gerald H. Anderson and Thomas Stranski, eds. (New York: Paulist Press, and Grand Rapids: Eerdmans, 1981), 157–58.

4. *Lumen Gentium*, 16, as quoted by Patrick Kalilombe, "The Salvific Value of African Religions" *AFER* 21, no. 3 (June 1979): 143.

5. "Salvation in African Traditional Religions," in *Voices from the Third World* 8, no. 4 (December 1985): 1–15.

6. *Old Testament Theology* (New York: Harper and Row, 1965), 2:121f., 129, 136.

7. D. N. Wambutda, "Savannah Theology: A Biblical Reconsideration of the Concept of Salvation in the African Context," in *Bulletin of African Theology* 3, no. 6 (July–December 1981): 146.

8. See *My Neighbor's Faith and Mine: Theological Discoveries through Interfaith Dialogue* (Geneva: World Council of Churches, 1986).

9. John Mbiti, *Bible and Theology in African Christianity* (Nairobi: Oxford University Press, 1986), 158–59.

10. Kalilombe, "The Salvific Value of African Religions," 156.

11. As quoted by John Mbiti in "Some Reflections on African Experience of Salvation Today," in *Living Faiths and Ultimate Goals*, ed. S. J. Samartha (Geneva: World Council of Churches, 1974), 111.

12. Ibid., 112–13.

13. See P. Tempels, *Bantu Philosophy*, Eng. trans. (Paris, 1959).

14. "Salvation in African Traditional Religions."

15. W. T. Harris and Harry Sawyerr, *The Springs of Mende Belief and Conduct* (Freetown: Sierra Leone University Press, 1968), 6–7.

16. In Samartha, ed., *Living Faiths and Ultimate Goals*, 115.

17. "Social Movement and the Role of Symbols," address at the Second Consultation of Christian Art in Asia, March 1984, as quoted in Masao Takenaka, *God Is Rice: Asian Culture and Christian Faith* (Geneva: World Council of Churches, 1986), 40.

18. See Dan Cohn-Sherbok, "Jewish-Christian Encounter and Liberation Theology," in *Common Ground*, nos. 1 and 2 (1987): 14–16.

19. Beyers Naudé and Dorothee Sölle, *Hope for Faith: A Conversation* (Geneva: WCC Publications, and Grand Rapids: Wm. B. Eerdmans, 1986), 31.

20. Ibid., 35.

21. *Hearing and Knowing: Theological Reflections on Christianity in Africa* (Maryknoll, N.Y.: Orbis Books, 1986), 107–8.

3

COVENANT WITH THE POOR: TOWARD A NEW CONCEPT OF ECONOMIC JUSTICE

Kim Yong-Bock

WHY ECONOMICS?

Our faith that God created the whole world and all its people means that all persons everywhere are the people of God. Any limitation of this all-inclusive notion of the people of God is a denial of the all-encompassing sovereignty of God over history, the universe, and the people therein. The people of God live within the socio-economic process of history, as testified by the biblical history of the Old and the New Testaments and church history. Therefore, it is necessary that theology discern the *political economy*[1] of the people of God, a political economy that is inherent in the history of humanity on earth. The covenant of God with the people of God thus has theoretical and practical implications for the political economy of all the peoples of the world. The "political economy of God" is in contrast to that of the worldly powers.

Christian faith and economics are not two separate categories; they are inseparable, and it is necessary to apply the spirit and teaching of Christ to economic and industrial life. The gospel is for all realms of life. The Christian faith cannot be reduced merely to an otherworldly realm and individual life, but should be concerned with the whole life of the people of God. Accordingly, the political economy of the people of God must be one of the central concerns of theology.[2]

Modern Economic Theories: Detached from Christian Faith

Christian faith is now being seriously tested with regard to its implications for the economic life of humanity in the context of the present international economic order of capitalism, socialism, and development. Economic theories have ruled out Christian faith as useful for any explanation of the economic life of humanity. Scientific reason has claimed autonomy and established self-authenticating theories in all the fields of scientific inquiry. Economic theories claim the same scientific autonomy.[3]

Christian theology has effectively withdrawn from the realm of economic life and economic science; it has relegated itself to a supramundane domain upon which it focuses its interest. Christian theology has isolated itself from the world and from the area of the sciences and theories about the life of this world. But this trend is both unbiblical and ahistorical and has created a crisis for theology, which no longer does any effective thinking about the economic life of the people.

In the West the secularization of economics since the Enlightenment has made economic theories independent of all theological and ethical considerations. This is true of both capitalist and socialist economic theories, neither of which has any real use for the Christian faith.

It is said that the autonomy of economics has been brought about by the philosophical development of rationalism and the treatment of economic life in scientific terms; by academic specialization; by the ascendancy of the economic doctrine of laissez faire; by the fragmentation of modern life, without any integration of values; and by the materialist understanding of history. Some theologians recognize that the role of Christian faith in God the creator has been decisive in the development of modern science.[4]

Moreover, economic power in the world today has become an *absolute entity*, needing no justification other than its unlimited and unrestricted power.[5] Economic theories are used to justify the existence of this power and its unlimited growth and expansion. The economic powers now dominating the world allow no place for the claim of the Christian faith for justice in determining the economic reality. This is not merely a question of the intelligibility of Christian beliefs or the social relevancy raised by Christian teaching on economics; rather, it is a historical denial and rejection of the "power" of Christian faith to shape the economic life of humanity.

In the Christian churches, some moral and ethical influence of faith on economics is accepted as it applies to individuals; the influence of faith in the corporate life of society is only generally recognized without specific theoretical expressions about the corporate reality.[6] In other words, the autonomy of economics and economic powers has been tacitly and liberally accepted. Therefore, the theoretical implications of the Christian faith for economic life have not been taken seriously and work on this issue has been grossly neglected.

Christian Faith and Capitalism

In fact, the history of Western theological development has been closely related to capitalist development. Max Weber's thesis has validity as a historical, not causal, explanation for the development of capitalism and its relation to the Protestant ethics of the West.[7] Christian ethics never disavowed this historical and ethical connection in either historical or ethical terms. Moreover, in many developing countries Christianity even boasts of its connection with Western capitalism as the agent of the modernization process.

Only recently has the question of economic life been taken seriously in relation to the Christian faith. The test of the Christian faith is its relation to the poor in the world, particularly in the Third World. Faith can be restored in the gospel of the poor and oppressed by going back to the biblical faith and articulating it in the present reality in the concrete terms of political economy.

The Christian socialist movements in the last two centuries have made insufficient progress in dealing with the question of the relationship between Christian faith and economic life, although these movements have criticized capitalist excesses.[8] The eighteenth- and nineteenth-century Christian socialists in England, the theologians of the Social Gospel, and the religious socialists of early twentieth-century Europe did not elaborate the implications of the Christian faith for political economy in human community. They carried out their prophetic function, but they failed to "incarnate" the Christian faith in the concrete economic life of the people and to meet the challenges of the capitalist and Marxist economic powers in theory and practice.

Christian theology has tacitly condoned capitalism and has reacted negatively to the socialist economy without examining its implications and relations with the Christian faith; and more seriously, the Christian faith has grossly neglected the proclamation of the gospel to the poor. The gospel to the poor has been distorted and even repudiated by Western Christianity, which is in captivity to the capitalist economic powers. For the same reason, the gospel to the poor was impoverished and never creatively shared with the people who live under the socialist state economy.

The capitalist economic powers have manifested themselves in global dimensions.[9] This is already shown in the reality of the giant transnational corporations, which seek to maximize their profits and to expand their power to control the world economy.[10] The unlimited expansion and concentration of economic power in its corporate and state-controlled forms is the major problem of humanity.[11]

Forthright criticism of the giant corporations has been very difficult, for they are closely associated with Christian churches in the West. When the World Council of Churches has taken a critical stance against large corporations in the West for their roles in South Africa and elsewhere in the Third World, it has caused a major controversy in the Western churches.[12]

Economic growth, conspicuous consumption, waste of resources, worship of mammon, division between rich and poor, injustice and exploitation, concentration of economic power and domination, ecological destruction, and cultural erosion are some of the symptoms of the present economic disorder, which makes the people spiritual victims as well.

In this kind of political economy the Christian faith is seriously challenged to witness to the gospel. Ecumenical efforts have made some progress; but there is still a long way to go to meet these challenges.[13]

Socialist State Economy and Christian Faith

It is widely claimed that the evils of capitalism can be overcome by a socialist economy. Communism has been the single greatest challenge to the Christian faith in terms of economic justice. But it has also been pointed out that economic collectivism is intolerable to the human spirit, which longs for freedom and creativity. Genuine community based on justice and *agape* should be established. The political economy of the socialist states has been politically dictatorial and economically collectivist, with property monopolized by the state power for planning, production, and distribution.

The monopoly of the state has been substituted in socialist economies for that of the giant corporations in the capitalist economies. The citizens are not allowed to participate in the planning, production, and distribution process; rather, the people are controlled in their own name. There has been no development of theological reflection on economic life as a witness to the gospel in the socialist states. The attitude of the churches, by and large, has been negative with regard to socialist developments. Churches in the socialist states are not in a position to witness to the reality of the gospel in politico-economic terms; this is due to historical reasons as well as to the church's own political status.

There have been developments and elaborations of the "socialist" political economic theories in different circumstances, and practical applications have been made in several Third World countries to varying extents. Some theologies have opted for such socialist theories and practices of political economy. This demands detailed examination that we cannot carry out here. It is not certain whether organic relations can be realized between the Christian faith and a socialist political economy of any sort.

The Christian Message:
Tested by the Poor and the Oppressed

The Christian faith is challenged by the poverty and suffering of the *minjung* (grassroots people). This challenge comes not only from the Marxist and capitalist powers in theory and practice, but also from the people themselves, the hungry and poor who are the majority of humanity, particularly in the Third World. Capitalists and their economic theories disdain the Christian faith for its irrelevance in seeking to rescue the poor. Socialists and their theories charge that the Christian faith justifies the capitalist rich.

The capitalist and socialist economies, in theory and practice, have not only been unable to meet the basic human needs in the Third World, but they have so exploited and oppressed the people that the poor and hungry are increasing and the world economic order is becoming more unjust and unstable, nearing a critical point in human history. In this context the relationship between the Christian faith and capitalism on the one hand and between the Christian faith and Marxist socialism on the other has become one of the most critical issues for the Christian churches and for Christian theologies.

Capitalism and Marxism have basically been left alone to dominate the thinking on political economy without any reference to the Christian faith. One excuse for this has been that the Christian faith has no interest in worldly affairs; another has been that the Christian faith cannot provide any "blueprint" for society. As a result of these attitudes Christian faith has tended not to be specific or concrete about the world political economy.

The conditions in the world, especially the plight of the poor, demand that the justice of God be done on earth as it is in heaven. The capitalist concept of justice has been deficient, despite its claim of equilibrium through free interaction of interests in the market place; and the socialist concept of justice has entailed the sacrifice of freedom under dictatorial rule. These socio-economic systems have undergone revisions, but without the major transformations needed to meet the demand of justice for the people of the world. The justice of God must be faithfully translated into the political economy of the *minjung*.

In the world economic order of capitalism, socialism, and massive and dire poverty, the Christian faith has been challenged in its theology and in its practical mission. The Western Christian churches have long been associated with capitalist development, due to their position in the capitalist economic order, with its social, political, and cultural implications. More often than is recognized, Christianity in the West has been influenced by capitalist power in its political theology. Christian churches in the world today have also reacted — or overreacted — to socialist developments and have withdrawn or been forced to withdraw from participation in socialist economic development. Of course, the formal argument has been that neither capitalism nor socialism can be regarded as a "Christian economic order."

Is not the gospel proclaimed to the poor? What does Christian faith say to the poor today? What is the concrete nature and content of the good news to the poor? What is the socio-economic content of the Christian faith? What is the nature of the political economy of God's reign?

"Man should not live by bread alone" — is this an answer? Or, "the Christian faith cannot give a detailed blueprint for the economic order, but it can provide a set of ethical criteria by which ethical judgments can be made in a given situation." Will a sort of middle axiom suffice for Christian social ethics? Justice, participation, peace, integrity of creation, and responsible society are ethical criteria for ecumenical actions in the world. Is providing such criteria a sufficient answer of the Christian faith that proclaims the good news to the poor? Still another response is that economics is a mundane arena of human life, and therefore only relative and tentative answers are available, or, that Christian faith can only provide moral principles for the life of the people, and these moral principles are differentiated and separated from socio-economic questions proper. Does the sovereign rule of God then have any implications for the political economy of the people of God on earth? If not, how does the gospel become good news to the poor, whose life is primarily conditioned by poverty?

The History of Theologies on Economic Questions

Cases of justification or criticism of private property are found in the history of Christian thought. Augustine defended private property as a punishment and partial remedy for original sin. This notion was attacked by the radical heretical movements of the Middle Ages and the Reformation. Aquinas insisted that private property was in accordance with natural law. Whereas the early fathers viewed it as a consequence of human sin, Luther and Calvin accepted private property as a legitimate condition of life in the order of creation as well as the Fall.

"Stewardship" was a widely accepted term among the Reformers as a response to the question of how to handle possessions. According to the Reformation, the right to use determines the right to possess. Rightly understood, possession is in order to use; use is not in order to possess (Lehmann). Use justifies possession. Puritanism and modern Catholicism (which regarded property as a sign that one was among the elect) accepted the highly individualistic notion, associated with laissez-faire capitalism, of the right to property as absolute and unconditional, and conceived of the state primarily as an instrument for the protection of this right.[14]

In the capitalist West, stewardship has been related only to the support of the church, not to the totality of life, nor to the resources of the earth. One-sided individualism has dominated through the doctrine of private property and through the control and self-regulation of self-interest through competition.

After the Industrial Revolution in Europe, there arose some Christian social traditions: charity work from the nineteenth century on; the movement for social legislation to protect workers; the Christian progressive associations and Christian socialists in the nineteenth century. These Christian groups were a minority within majority Christendom.[15]

But these traditions did not provide an alternative for the poor working classes in Europe and North America, perhaps because they did not emerge from among the poor Christians themselves. Christian social ideas were largely the product of Christian elites who were concerned with the victims of industrialization. It was not their concern to spell out the "political economy" of the reign of God in the context of capitalist development. Secular thinkers such as Karl Marx did try to work out an alternative political economy to supplant the capitalist development, although I make this point not to endorse the Marxist alternative.

While such theologians as Emil Brunner grounded the right to private property on the right of freedom and thus endorsed capitalism, Karl Barth, Paul Tillich, Reinhold Niebuhr, and others sought to criticize capitalist development on a religious basis without working out any concrete political economy of religious socialism.[16]

Liberation theologies and the Christians for Socialism movement in the Third World have accepted class analysis, class struggle, and some degree of socialism, though the concrete character of this socialism is not well clarified. Theirs is an effort to reconcile the Christian faith with Marxist economic thought, in its many variations. It is an unanswered question whether the political economy of Marxist socialism can be an expression of the "political economy" of the reign of God in a particular Third World situation. A key problem is the nature of the relationship between the Christian faith and "scientific" Marxism.

Still, modern Christian ethicists in general justify the capitalist economy in the following fashion:

> Within the context of absolute ownership by God alone, biblical faith assumes the necessity of some measure of individual ownership, although it is keenly aware of the

moral and social dangers of wealth, and imposes severe limitations upon its acquisition and use in order to protect the welfare of less fortunate persons as well as that of society as a whole. In the Old Testament, the very existence of the commandment "You shall not steal" presupposes the right of individual ownership. Similarly, frequent protests made by prophets against the infringement of the prohibition of stealing implies that they assumed that right of individuals to own property. Also in the New Testament, some measure of private ownership is presupposed as normal. Even the communism of love which was practiced for a time at Jerusalem after Pentecost (Acts 2:44–45; 5:1–5) does not provide an exception to this rule, for all were free either to place or not to place their property at the disposal of the community; moreover, there is no evidence that such communal sharing of goods was followed in the other Christian communities. This practice at Jerusalem seems to have been looked upon as a product of Christian fellowship rather than as a blueprint for the economic order.[17]

Christian theology has not met the demands of the gospel in terms of the spelling out of Christian faith for the political economy of the people; and therefore, the Christian churches have not been able to meet the challenges of the *minjung* in their poverty and suffering.

It is not sufficient to be morally critical of the existing political economies that dominate the world economic order. It is not sufficient to formulate certain ethical guidelines for the churches and Christian groups to act on economic issues.[18] These are necessary. However, the historical crisis is that both the socialist and the capitalist options have been played out, and that the poverty and suffering of the people are continuing into the foreseeable future. In this situation Christian theology should not only liberate itself from its enslavement to the present world economic order, but should also work out concrete political-economic theory and practice, based on the Christian community's living out and witnessing to the sovereign *oikonomia* of God for the people of God.[19]

POLITICAL ECONOMY
OF THE SOVEREIGNTY OF GOD

God's covenant with the poor is not merely to secure the socio-economic life of the poor but also to guarantee the *shalom* of the human community for the fullness of life. This is the socio-economic manifestation of the sovereignty of God over life on earth.

Here we want to explore the biblical basis for God's covenant(ing) with the poor. The objective is not to translate into economics directly and immediately the directions that may emerge from our biblical reflections, but to read out some implications for the socio-economic life of the people.

We may begin with the story of the slaves in the Bible as the context of the covenant with the poor. Slavery was the central socio-economic institution of biblical times, from the period of the Egyptian pharaohs to the Roman empire.[20] The relevance of the story of the slaves to the contemporary world is not immediate or direct; yet, from a poor people's point of view, social subjugation in work and life is still a pressing reality. The poor suffer some sort of slavery in the socio-economic sense. This is the nature of work and labor relations.

The Political Economy of Slavery

The story of Yahweh begins with the story of the slaves in Egypt. The social biography of the slave is paradigmatic in the Bible as well as in human history. The culmination of God's saving action is to deliver the slaves from the bondage of the Egyptian empire and to establish a community of the people that is free of such social bondage. The Hebrew slaves were liberated from their bondage and were led to build a community in covenant with Yahweh, the legislated form of which appears in Exodus 21, Leviticus 15, and Deuteronomy 15. These different versions of the covenant laws are based on differences in historical conditions.

The story of the Hebrew slaves is as follows:

The Egyptians forced the sons of Israel into slavery, and made their lives unbearable with hard labor, work with clay and with brick, all kinds of work in the fields; they forced on them every kind of labor. The king of Egypt then spoke to the Hebrew midwives.... "When you midwives attend Hebrew women," he said, "watch the two stones carefully. If it is a boy, kill him; and if a girl, let her live...." The sons of Israel, groaning in their slavery, cried out for help and from the depths of their slavery their cry came up to God. God heard their groaning...and Yahweh said, "I have seen the miserable state of my people in Egypt. I have heard their appeal to be free of their slave drivers. Yes. I am very well aware of their suffering." (Exod. 1–3)

The core of the story of the Hebrew slaves in Egypt appears here very clearly. There are the Hebrew slaves, Yahweh of the Hebrews, and the Egyptian power in the form of imperial ruler, slave drivers, and military might. In this story the protagonist is the Hebrew slaves; Yahweh takes sides in a special relationship with the Hebrews; Yahweh becomes the partner in covenant with the Hebrew slaves, who are now the people of God.

The story of the slaves reveals the Egyptian socioeconomic structure and its exploitation and oppression of the people as well as the nature of Egyptian power and its system of rule. The historical details of the Egyptian state cannot be known; nevertheless the biblical account clearly reveals the nature of the antagonist in the story. It exposes the core of the political economy of the Egyptian empire.

The political economy of the Egyptian pharaoh was that of a hydraulic civilization, where massive public works and civil engineering and construction skills were required to control water resources. In this system of political economy a large slave labor force and a strong and central bureaucracy were necessary. The toils of the Hebrew slaves must be understood in this context.

The pharaoh, Ramses II, was afraid of the increasing numbers of the Hebrews and felt, "If war breaks out, they might add to the number of our enemies. They might take arms against us and so escape out of the country"

(Exod. 1:10). The pharaoh ordered the killing of the innocent male Hebrew babies, commanding, "Throw all the boys born to the Hebrews into the river" (Exod. 1:22). He was engaged in building projects such as the great supply cities of Pithom and Ramses, which was his own residence (Exod. 1:11). When the call of Moses came, "Let my people go,"

> Pharaoh gave this command to the people's slave drivers and to the overseers, "Up to the present, you have provided these people with straw for brick making. Do so no longer; let them go and gather straw for themselves. All the same you are to get from them the same number of bricks as before, not reducing it at all. They are lazy, and that is why their cry is, 'Let us go and offer sacrifice to our God.' Make these men work harder than ever, so that they do not have time to stop and listen to glib speeches."

Pharaoh did not let the people go till the bitter end, for he did not recognize the authority of Yahweh. Ramses II held the absolute authority of the oriental despot, calling himself a son of the sun goddess.

The central point of the story is the liberation of the Hebrew slaves from the Egyptian political economy. Yahweh liberated them from their bondage in Egypt. Yahweh was the God of the Hebrew slaves, and the Hebrew slaves were the people of Yahweh. This relationship was a liberating one for the Hebrew slaves; and on this basis there rose the Sinai covenant of mutual faithfulness, that is, as long as the Hebrews were faithful to their God, Yahweh would protect them from the bondage of slavery.

This is the central core of the Old Testament message. This paradigmatic experience of the Hebrew people gave birth to the covenant code, in Exodus 21:1–23:33, the heart of which is the legislation on the liberation of slaves. This legislation forms the political economy of the liberated community.

This had far-reaching implications for the people of God in the empires of Babylonia and Assyria, and in other states and subsequent empires, as well as for the development of the socio-political order of the people of God.

Who were the Hebrew slaves? It is clearly established that the name "Israel" was not given to the Hebrews in Egypt and in the wilderness; it was attributed to the community of the Hebrews in Palestine when they formed a confederacy. Recent scholarly discussions show that the term 'apiru has a close affinity to the name "Hebrew." 'Apiru is a state labor force, composed of captured people, purchased people, and other slaves. The phenomenon of 'apiru was widespread in the Near Eastern civilization of biblical times. We may conclude that the Hebrew slaves were representative of all those 'apiru and other socially bondaged people.

Who became a slave? The origin of slavery was fundamentally socio-economic. Inability to repay a debt meant one was forced to pay it by slave labor. Thus insolvency was one of the basic origins of slavery. Mesopotamian laws, such as the code of Hammurabi and the Middle Assyrian laws, recognized the right of the creditor to seize his defaulting debtor and force him into compulsory service. This practice was widespread in Palestine as well.

One of the earliest sources of slavery was war. Captives of war, and in some cases also large segments of the defeated population, were reduced to slavery. Another source of slavery was slave trade. This was carried out not only internationally, but also in the form of the sale of minors, for example, the sale of children by their parents, especially in times of economic stress. Hunger and debt drove people to sell first their children and then themselves.

Thus Hebrew slavery originated in hunger and debt, war and captivity. The slaves were treated as commodities to be sold, bought, leased, exchanged, or inherited. Female slaves were leased for work, given as a pledge, or handed over as a part of a dowry. In addition to their routine duties as maidservants, they were subject also to burdens peculiar to their sex. Ownership of a female slave meant not only the right to employ her physical strength, but also, and in many cases primarily, the exploitation of her charms by the male members of her master's household and the utilization of her body for the breeding of slave children. The highest position a female slave could achieve was to become a childbearing concubine of her master, and the lowest, to be used as a professional prostitute. Slavery occurred also in the post-Exodus life of the people of God as well as throughout the ancient Near East. The slavery system was entrenched in the life of the Hebrew people. This was the result of economic and social dealings within the Hebrew community, and it was reinforced and expanded by the establishment of state slavery and the institution of corvée upon the emergence of the strong and centralized power of Kings David and Solomon.

The Political Economy of the Covenant

Such is the context in which the Yahweh of the Hebrew slaves concretely intervened in history, in the Exodus; this intervention was structuralized as the covenant at Mt. Sinai, and the Exodus experience became an integral part of Hebrew history. Thus, covenant codes were developed to protect the liberated community in which there were no slaves. These legislations, which are found in Exodus 21, Leviticus 25, and Deuteronomy 15, are codes against slavery and for the rights of slaves to be free from the Egyptian and other imperial and feudal powers of enslavement in the Near East.

The text of the earliest covenant code, found in Exodus 21:1–11, should be understood in the context of the liberated community of the Hebrew people, who had been slaves in Egypt. It is an order radically different from the other legislation on slavery of the ancient Near East, which was to maintain and regulate the slavery system. The covenant code was to liberate and protect the rights of slaves. "In the seventh year he may leave; he shall be free, with no compensations to pay" (Exod. 21:2). This was to establish the basic security of the Hebrew community against the powers of domination. This legislation was reinstated again and again, and the people of Israel were reminded of it on innumerable occasions throughout history.

All through the history of Israel, the renewal of the

covenant meant the liberation of slaves, though in actual practice this was not always carried out. For example, during the prophecy of Jeremiah, King Zedekiah made a pact with all the people in Jerusalem to free their slaves. All the nobles and all the people who entered the pact agreed that everyone should free his slaves, both men and women. This pact was later disavowed by the people. The point, however, is that the covenant meant liberation of the Hebrew slaves.

The covenant gave the right to Hebrew slaves to be freed from their slavery at the Sabbath year, and female slaves who did not have any means of survival were guaranteed the rights of food, clothing, and even conjugal relations (Exod. 21:1-11).

The community of liberated Hebrew slaves in ancient Palestine was protected by the covenant against homicide, injury, theft, and various economic offenses involving illicit transfer of properties and goods.

The covenant protected the weak, virgins, strangers, widows and orphans, and even animals. The covenant to protect the people was extended also to the enemy (Exod. 23:4). In the covenant the poor and the weak were protected in terms of their basic bodily, socio-economic, moral, and religious security from violations by the powerful forces of enslavement and injury.

The covenantal protection involved life and health as well. "You are to worship Yahweh your God, and I will bless your bread and water, and remove sickness from among you. In your land no woman will miscarry, none be barren. I will give you your full term of life" (Exod. 23:25, 26). Furthermore, the covenant involved feasts for the protection of the covenant community from cultural poverty and religious idolatry.

The covenant community of the former Hebrew slaves was promised land, including vineyards and olive groves. The land use was not only to secure food for the community but also to protect the poor and even helpless animals, who were also covenant partners of Yahweh. The slaves and the work animals were protected from overwork by the Sabbath laws (Exod. 23:10, 11).

The land was granted by God to secure the life of the people of God; it was promised to the tribes of Israel for their security and prosperity, and no transfer of property, especially inherited land, to other tribes or to outsiders could be made. This was a form of guarantee of the socioeconomic security of the people of God (Num. 36:5–9).

Furthermore, the changing of the boundaries of the allotted land was not permissible, for these boundaries had been set to protect the property of the tribes of Yahweh. A curse was put upon any person who displaced his neighbor's land boundary mark (Deut. 27:17). Any commercial transfer of land was prohibited, and the transfer of land to a debtor could not be permanent even in intratribal dealings. According to the sabbatical law, land should be made available to the poor in the Sabbath year, for their protection (Exod. 23:10–11 and Lev. 25:1–7).

In the year of Jubilee, the whole state of affairs should be restored to its original situation as Yahweh had intended. "You must put my laws and customs into practice; you must keep them, practice them; and so you shall be secure in your possession of the land. The land will give its fruits, you will eat your fill and live in security" (Lev. 25:18–19). Here is confirmation that the land is for the socio-economic security of the people of God.

In the year of Jubilee the transferred land should be redeemed by the originally allotted party. "Land must not be sold in perpetuity, for the land belongs to me, and to me you are only strangers and guests. You will allow a right of redemption on all your landed property" (Lev. 25:23–24).

In the story of Naboth's vineyard, Naboth refuses to sell his vineyard to King Ahab, answering Ahab, "Yahweh forbid that I should give you the inheritance of my ancestors" (1 Kings 21:3). It is clear that no land transfer is allowed, for that would threaten the very security of the people, guaranteed by God against poverty and enslavement in the covenant.[21]

Nevertheless, the history of the kingdoms of the people of Israel was subverted by ways of life and socio-economic structures in which poverty and enslavement were bound to rise. An example is found in the introduction of kingship into the life of the people of Israel. Kingship, founded upon the rulers' socio-economic domination of the people, inevitably resulted in the poverty and enslavement of the population, as the book of Samuel testifies (1 Sam. 8:10–22). This is shown again in the story of the prophet Nathan's rebuke of King David, and in Jezebel's execution of Naboth in order to take over his vineyard. The prophets speak out against this kind of violation of justice that creates distorted social relations and economic domination.

In other words, the covenant is for the socio-economic protection and security of the enslaved and poor people of God from the beginning to the end of their history. The covenant code and the subsequent legal developments and prophetic movements must be seen in the context of God's covenant with the Hebrew slaves, and with those like them in other historical circumstances: the poor, orphans, strangers, widows, and others who are unprotected and insecure in socio-economic terms.

The prophetic movements of Elijah, Micah, and Amos protested the breaking of the covenant and demanded restoration of the covenant relationship to protect justice and the rights of the poor, for the restoration of the socio-economic security of the people of God as a whole. During the monarchic period, even though the covenantal framework was accepted in society, it was broken by injustices in the political and socio-economic structure and the life of the kingdoms.[22]

But the covenantal framework of the people's life could not be maintained at all under the conditions of exile in Babylon or Assyria, or under the circumstances of "colonial" domination by the Greek and Roman empires. Therefore, the people of God became preoccupied with the restoration of the covenant relationship with Yahweh in its concrete religious and socio-economic manifestations. For this reason the restoration of the political life of the people of Israel was critically important. The conditions of their life under the Exile and colonial domination can be compared to the life of a lamb in the jungle, fought over by wild beasts.

In the New Testament, the new covenant has usually been understood in spiritual terms only, but such an understanding is completely unwarranted. In the first place, recognition of the political and socio-economic context of the new covenant is essential to understand the life of the community of the faithful. The macro-structure of the Roman empire was an economy based on the slavery system, both in the production of agricultural goods and in the life of the urban elites. We will not discuss here the details of socio-economic life in the Roman empire and Palestine. When the life of the new covenant, the community of the faithful, is seen in the context of the Roman empire, then the socio-economic implications of the life of the early Christian community can be clarified. This is no longer a monarchic situation. It is life under the colonial domination of the Roman empire.

Jesus restates the finality of the covenant relationship in his summary of the covenant between God and the people of God: love your God and love your neighbor as yourself. The life of Jesus with the multitudes (*ochlos*) is to restore the rule of God among them, that is, to restore the covenant of God with the people. The unmistakable concern of Jesus for the poor, the sick, the weak, and social outcasts is the mark of the restoration of the covenant: the socio-economic security of the people under God's rule. The eschatological intensity of Jesus' concern should not allow the transcendentalization or futurization of the issue; rather, it should be understood as the urgency of restoration, the imminent coming of the reign of God, which would bring the radical breakdown of Roman domination and the restoration of the new covenant community of the faithful.

For example, in chapter 6 of the gospel according to Matthew, Jesus teaches on the major economic issues of daily bread, socio-economic security of the poor, and mammonism. Almsgiving is a natural consequence of the covenant, and therefore nothing to boast of (Matt. 6:1–4). Daily bread is the first human demand in the Lord's Prayer, and redemption of the indebted is its central concern. Economic asceticism is not proper to the poor, and accumulation of wealth is permissible only under the sovereign rule of God; otherwise it will corrupt and will be subject to thievery. God and money are mutually exclusive as objects of worship. Finally, socio-economic security is dependent upon God, and therefore the most fundamental issue is the establishment of the just rule of God. This economic outlook is none other than the political economy of the covenant.

The most dramatic expression of the socio-economic dimension of the new covenant is found in the early church, especially in Acts 2:42–47 and 4:32–5:11. This is the protection of the community of the faithful, who are the new people of God: "The faithful lived together and owned everything in common; they sold their goods and possessions and shared out the proceeds among themselves according to what each needed." "None of their members was ever in want." That is, there were no poor.

Often this powerful, dynamic socio-economic reality of the early church has been ignored or dismissed as eschatological or utopian. But this was the reality, to be seen in the context of the political economy of the Roman empire. The early church radically challenged the entire socio-economic system, which was based upon slavery. This is why masterless slaves and freedmen were drawn into the Christian community, and why it was regarded as subversive by the Roman authorities. The letters of St. Paul and his social teachings must be understood in this context. For example, his letter to Philemon and his reference to Christ as slave in the letter to the Philippians (chapter 2) obviously had profound socio-economic implications in the Roman empire. These cannot be viewed as eschatological or individual ethical teachings.

The Story of the Poor and Prophetic Economics

The covenant between Yahweh and the people was essentially to protect the rights of the poor, a basic guarantee for the liberated community of the Exodus. Thus the story of the poor became the central focus of the involvement of Yahweh in the history of the people of Israel. It is here that the prophetic movement finds its proper place.

Who were the poor? They were those who were destitute of material possessions in the society. The poor formed a much broader social stratum than the slaves, and their antagonists included the rich, as is well illustrated in the speech of Nathan to David. Widows were poor, having no right of inheritance, and were the objects of harsh treatment. In close association with widows, the fatherless were regarded as poor — especially the fatherless daughter, who had no inheritance, unless her father had no sons. It has been suggested that the "fatherless" were the female children of sacred prostitutes, who had no identifiable father. Sojourners also were included among the poor, for they did not have the protection and benefits that were usually taken for granted in their native lands. They were people who had escaped natural calamities, wars, and other disasters in their native places, who lived outside their native communities. They were refugees. The people of Israel regarded themselves as having once been sojourners in Egypt. Sojourners were classified in the same status as widows and orphans and were totally dependent upon acceptance by the community, which determined whether they were invited in.

Thus, the poor are those who are economically destitute — because of their loss of property or their lack of inheritance, or because of their having been robbed by the powerful and rich.

In biblical literature the poor are defended by the covenant codes, by legal statutes, and by the prophets. The poor are truly the central figures in the historical drama that unfolds between Yahweh and the people of Israel. The poor are the protagonists; the rich and powerful are the antagonists. The rich are identified with the wicked: "seizing the field that they covet, they take over houses as well, owner and house they confiscate together, taking both man and inheritance" (Mic. 2:2).

The poor have a special place in the covenant relationship between God and the people of Israel, just as the slaves were protagonists in liberation history. The poor are a special charge of God in the Old Testament. God, through the Mosaic legislation and the prophetic exhortations, seeks social justice for the poor (Deut. 10:17–18; 2 Sam. 22:28; Isa. 25:4; Amos 2:6; 4:1, etc.). Many laws concerning the poor are found in Leviticus 19 and 23 and Deuteronomy 14–15 and 25. The poor have a special "privilege" in the covenant community, and it is not merely an eschatological one. Widows, the fatherless, sojourners, and other weak people are protected; and the Hebrew judges are to give the poor full protection (Exod. 23:3; Deut. 16:19; Ps. 82:3, etc.).

The poor have a special and privileged status under the messianic reign. The gospel is given to the poor, whereas anathema is often preached to the rich and powerful dominators. In the prophecy of Isaiah it is written, "The spirit of the Lord Yahweh has been given to me, for Yahweh has anointed me. He has sent me to bring good news to the poor " (Isa. 61:1).

Against the tyranny of the rich, the prophet Micah proclaims,

> So Yahweh says this: Now it is I who plot such mischief against this breed as your neck will not escape; nor will you be able to walk proudly, so evil will the time be. On that day they will make a satire on you, sing a dirge and say, "We are stripped of everything; my people's portion is measured out and shared, no one will give it back to them, our fields are awarded to our despoiler." Therefore you will have no one to measure out a share in the community of Yahweh. (Mic. 2:3–5)

And Hosea proclaims,

> Canaan holds fraudulent scales in his hands, to defraud is his delight. "How rich I have become!" says Ephraim, "I have amassed a fortune." But he will keep nothing of all his profits, because of the guilt that he has brought on himself. (Hos. 12:8–9)

Isaiah laments the situation of Jerusalem,

> What a harlot she has become, the faithful city, Zion, that was all justice! Once integrity lived there, now assassins. Your silver has turned into dross, your wine is watered.

Your princes are rebels, accomplices of thieves. All are
greedy for profits and chase after bribes. They show no
justice to the orphan, the cause of the widow is never
heard. (Isa.1:21–23)

In the New Testament the poor are given an even more
prominent status: the poor occupy the central place in the
messianic reign — that is, the reign of God. Jesus pro-
nounces, "How happy are you who are poor: yours is the
kingdom of God. Happy are you who are hungry now:
you shall be satisfied....But alas for you who are rich:
you are having consolation now. Alas for you who have
your fill now: you shall go hungry" (Luke 6:20, 21, 24, 25).
Jesus lived among the poor, unconditionally in communion
with them, sharing the good news of the reign of God. In
the experience of the early church Jesus established an
eschatological identity with the poor and hungry (Matt.
25:31–46). Indeed, the poor are the privileged guests at
the messianic banquet (Matt. 22:1–14; Luke 14:15–24).

Let us look at the "economics" of Luke, which focuses
on socio-economic protection of the poor. In Luke's economy, "the hungry he has filled with good things, the rich
sent away" (Luke 1:53), as sung by Mary. Jesus encoun-
ters the economic issue (Luke 4:4) and contradicts the
devil with the economy of manna, which is fulfillment
of God's covenant with the hungry Hebrews (Deut. 8:3).
Eating and drinking with the poor is a divine feast for
Jesus (Luke 5:29–32). The feeding of the hungry is a law
superior to the Pharisaic religious regulations (Luke 6:5).
How happy are you who are poor: yours is the kingdom
of God. Happy you who are hungry now: you shall be
satisfied (Luke 6:20). The economics of Luke is very radical: "Give to everyone who asks you, and do not ask for
your property back from the man who robs you" (Luke
6:30). How can we deny that the economics of the miracle of the loaves is that of sharing (Luke 9:12–17)? The
story of the Good Samaritan is the story of the robbed
and the people who are made poor and God's promise to protect them (Luke 10:29ff.). The invitation to the
messianic feast is made to the poor (Luke 14:15ff.). The

privilege of the poor man Lazarus in God's reign is very clear (Luke 16:19ff.). The centrality of the ten command- ments (the Law) is to "sell all that you own and distribute the money to the poor, and you will have treasure in heaven" (Luke 18:18ff.). Jesus praises the poor widow for her total commitment to the lordship of God in her eco- nomic life (Luke 21:1ff.). Luke's testimony to the early life of the church demonstrates that the economic life of the community of the faithful was one of total sharing, so that there was no person in the community who was poor.

Covenant for Life

The story of the creation is the story of God's covenant for life on earth against the power of death of the political economy of the "Babylonian empire." It is the covenant of God with the oppressed people of God, whose life was threatened with extinction. It is the affirmation of faith in the sovereignty of God over all creation, the center of which is life.

The power of the imperial domination was mythically identified as a state of "formless void" and "darkness over the deep" (Gen. 1:1). Therefore, the source and the begin- ning of life and the earth cannot be found in the primeval chaos (Tiamat) of Babylonian cosmogony, which is the "ideology" of the imperial power. This imperial power is often identified as Leviathan or Rahab, a monster from the deep sea (Job 9:13; Isa. 27:1; 51:9, etc.). The story of faith in the Creator of heaven and earth should be understood as the political economy of God vs. that of the imperial powers, which claim absolute rule over the whole cosmos.

With the Babylonian rule of Tiamat (goddess of chaos) as background, the political economy of God the Creator of heaven and earth, and of life therein, unfolds in the stories of creation in Genesis 1 and 2, in Psalm 104, and in Second Isaiah. God's political economy is the garden of creation, preservation, protection, and securing of life and its fullness, that is, *shalom:*

And God blessed them, and God said to them, "Be fruitful and multiply, and fill the earth and subdue it; and have dominion over the fish of the sea and over the birds of the air and over every living thing that moves upon the earth." And God said, "Behold, I have given you every plant yielding seed which is upon the face of all the earth, and every tree with seed in its fruit; you shall have them for food. (Gen. 1:28–29)

And the Lord planted a garden in Eden...and out of the ground the Lord God made to grow every tree that is pleasant to the sight and good for food, the tree of life also in the midst of the garden....A river flowed out of Eden to water the garden....The Lord took the man and put him in the garden of Eden to till and keep it. (Gen. 2:8–15)

God's blessing and call to "be fruitful and multiply" is the expression of God's sovereignty, which guarantees the life of the people of God. The creating of the garden and the placing of humans in it is another expression of God's sovereignty over the earth. The conflict between Cain and Abel leads to destruction of human life, and the flood is the cause of the destruction of all life. Therefore, God made the covenant of life with the people of Israel:

And God blessed Noah and his sons, and said to them, "Be fruitful and multiply, and fill the earth....Every moving thing that lives shall be food for you; and as I give the green plants, I give you every thing. Only you shall not eat flesh with life, that is its blood....Whoever sheds the blood of man, by man shall his blood be shed....Behold, I establish my covenant with you and your descendants after you, and with every living creature that is with you....I establish my covenant with you, that never again shall all flesh be cut off by the waters of a flood, and never again shall there be a flood to destroy the earth....This is the sign of the covenant I make between me and you and every living creature that is with you, for all future generations: I set my bow in the cloud, and it shall be a sign of covenant between me and the earth...." (Gen. 9:1–17)

This is the covenant between God and God's creation to protect life on earth, human and otherwise. It is expressed again in Revelation 21 and 22. This is an important dimension of the covenant that permeates the entire Bible.

God as the Gardener of Life

In the story of God we hear the cry of the people who are victimized by the Leviathan, the Dinosaur, and the Leopard in the jungle and desert. In the story of the Exodus we hear the cry of the Hebrew slaves who are victimized by the construction projects of the pharaoh. In the story of the Suffering Servant in Isaiah 53, there is the cry of the captives and exiles under the Babylonian and Assyrian empires. We see the dry bones in the valley of political domination in the dream of Ezekiel (Ezek. 37). We view the scene of Daniel as he is thrown into the den of lions, symbolizing the fate of the people of God under the Greek empire. We hear the lamentations of Rachel over Herod's massacre of innocent babes in Bethlehem under the tyranny of the Roman empire. The story of the crucifixion of Jesus of Nazareth is the cry of humanity from the midst of the jungle. The vision of Revelation 13 amplifies the reality of the power of the Roman empire.

The victims of the Leopards and Leviathans are the people, for whom God cares. God created the garden and God is the Gardener, and God has made humans according to God's image, that is, as gardeners. God's saving work is to transform jungle and desert into a garden, full of justice, freedom, love, and *shalom*. In the divine garden there is true integrity of creation.

The story of the creation, centered in the garden, is the overcoming of the chaos of the jungle. The vision of Isaiah the prophet (Isa. 11:1–9) is none other than that of the garden. John's vision (Rev. 21:1–4) is the city garden, where God dwells with the people of God. The planting and cultivating of a life of justice and *shalom* is God's very act of dwelling with the people. The death and the resurrection of Jesus the Messiah is the overcoming of the jungle of death and the recovery of the garden of life. The story of the creation is not the tale of the beginning of the world, but that of the victory of God's garden over the jungle of chaos and domination. Likewise, the eschatological vision of Revelation 21 is the overcoming of the Leviathan and the dwelling of God with the people of God in justice and peace and in harmony with the universe. The oppression of the tower of Babel, in the center of the jungle, has been overthrown by the act of the Holy Spirit to create communion (*koinonia*) and communication. This is the great beginning of the Christian church — the communion of saints who are the gardeners of love, justice, and peace in the created order of God: "And the Lord God took the man, and put him into the garden of Eden to dress it and to keep it" (Gen. 2:15).

One of the great concerns for humanity has been how to deal with the natural environment, for nature has been the "source of human life," as well as a threat to life at times. In recent years this concern has become focused sharply on a new problem, that is, the advancement of human ability to control and manipulate the natural forces by means of science and technology has created a situation where life is threatened by pollution, nuclear weapons, and the unforeseen consequences of intervention in the natural processes.

The issue of the relationship between human life and nature is not merely the question of how to deal with the natural environment but that of the total creation, which involves justice, participation, and peace in an integrated unity. One warning on the use of these terms is in order: theologically, the term "creation" does not refer only to nature, but to the whole creation, human and otherwise. Sometimes there has been confusion between the terms "creation" and "nature." Nature is only a part of creation. The theological notion of creation expresses the relationship between God and the whole reality. God's act of creation is over against the power of darkness, formlessness, and chaos, symbolized by the "Babylonian power." It is God's saving and liberating act for the whole of creation. In Second Isaiah God is the author of a new creation, a new beginning of earth, heaven, and life, from within the Babylonian chaos of imperial power (Isa. 51:9–11). In the same way, Christ is the author of a new creation. God created heaven and earth through Christ. Against the background of the Roman empire, the Book of Revelation tells the stories of messianic combat against the power of Satan, while the political economy of Rome (Rev. 18) and the political economy of the messianic reign (Rev. 21, 22) are juxtaposed to show that the new creation is a concrete political economy of life.

The Pauline and Johannine literature confirm the basic faith in the new creation, which means the political economy of new life. The act of creation is God's covenant with the people of God for their life, and so the new covenant for new life is realized in Christ. The christological passages of John 1:14, Colossians 1:15, 2 Corinthians 5:1, 7, etc., should be understood in the context of the political economy of new creation. The decisive battle is being waged between the political economy of the cosmos, where (imperial) Satan rules, and the political economy of the messianic reign on earth.

It has been said that the Bible does not speak about economic issues directly; or even if it does, that it is irrelevant for contemporary economic life. On the contrary, a straightforward reading of the Bible stories finds them speaking fundamental truths about the economic issues of property, production, and distribution for the life of the people of God in biblical times — and with direct bearing upon the fundamental issues of political economy in the contemporary world.

COVENANT WITH THE MINJUNG

The affirmation that God is in covenant with the people of God — who are the poor, the equivalent of the slaves — is not simple to translate into practice today. Nevertheless, the implications of such a covenant must be clarified in the present socio-economic context.

In any nation, the socio-economic context cannot be

separated from the political process, nor can it be separated from the global political economy. I have used two symbols for the existing political economy: Dinosaur and Leviathan. The Dinosaur represents the giant corporation or economic system that aims at infinite growth, while the Leviathan stands for the state that seeks its survival (security) through all possible means, however destructive they may be.

The world's economic systems, including both private capitalism and corporate (including state) capitalism, exploit humans and natural resources, causing immense suffering and devastation and creating injustice and imbalance in every society in the world. The political powers and regimes that undergird the economic systems are oppressive structures that deny the participation of the people and relegate them to objecthood. The nation-states are engaged in the arms race to maximize their security on the basis of their power to destroy each other. This threatens the peace and survival of humanity.

Thus, if one views global and national situations as the habitat of the Dinosaurs and Leviathans, then the world and its societies are seen as one big jungle, where the poor and weak cannot survive. In this context the covenant of God with the poor and weak has critical importance for the destiny of humankind and the created world.

It is clear that the systems of the state and of economic production, which were designed to protect humanity, are threatening the very life of the people (*minjung*); therefore we must discover the process by which the covenant of God with the *minjung* can be concretized in historical terms to guarantee their security.

God's covenant partner is the poor, just as it was the Hebrew slaves in Egypt. The poor are not merely the object of charity, welfare, or even economic distribution. They have rights and duties to God in the framework of the covenant. Here the important issue is how the churches and ecumenical movement recognize the subjecthood of the poor, who are in covenant with God. The churches may explore the possibility of concrete partnerships with organizations of the people (*minjung*), such as community organizations of the poor, basic ecclesial communities, and people's movements, in which the subjecthood of the people is asserted and even realized to a great extent.

The concrete objective of the covenant is to realize the justice and faithfulness of God, who is in covenant with the poor, protecting their socio-economic security from all kinds of slavery and liberating them from the systems of "pharaoh." The Dinosaurs and Leviathans must be expelled from the jungle, and the historical logic of survival of the fittest, security by all destructive means, and absolutization of political power will have to disappear from the garden of God, that is, the community of the people of God. This means that some concrete articulation of the vision of human community is needed. The fundamental clue for this is not in social philosophy or the social sciences, but in the covenant of God with the poor, which is the promise of God to secure the people of God from "slavery" throughout all ages.

This covenant relationship with the poor, in turn, will begin to clarify the relationship of the churches with the corporate powers and the states and their military establishments. Whenever these power entities and their systems ignore and even obstruct the covenant of God with the poor, failing to respect the covenant relationships of the churches with the poor and even hindering these, they will have to be denounced. The very foundation of the state, the economic productive process, and all security arrangements must be directed toward realizing the justice of God, to protect the poor, the people (*minjung*) of God.

The common life and *koinonia* of the first Christian communities were not a romantic version of utopia, but the absolute mandate of God and the genuine manifestation of the experience of the new covenant in the Spirit. For so long we have dismissed these fundamental manifestations of the life and community of the people of God in the old and new covenants.

It is high time for the communities of the faithful to restore the covenant of God with the *minjung* and to enter into the covenanting process with the poor. As communities of the faithful, we need to read the Bible more faithfully than ever; and we must mobilize all the wisdom we can — from all quarters, from the historical experiences of the churches to religious and secular experiences — in order to find the footprints of God's covenant with the poor.

Covenant with the Minjung: The People Will Overcome

God has promised the *minjung* that they will be secure in a full and whole life; and the *minjung* must believe that God is faithful and just. This is the content and format of the covenant. The *minjung* are the covenant partner of God, and no power or being can subvert this covenant.

Going back to the people means that we must believe that the people are the subjects of their own history, the partners of God in history, not the objects of political and economic rule by the rich and powerful. One might say that the people are powerless and poor, and this is objectively true. Because of their powerlessness and poverty, they are inherently not committed to the present regime of the political economy and, therefore, are able to seek a transcendent future perspective. Their disfranchisement, their experience of dispossession, and their social dislocation make them free of the central power authority and of the power of the monopoly; and their experience of political repression, economic exploitation, and social injustice makes them rise up to struggle against the regime. The people are true inheritors of the future, and they yearn for the vindication of justice. They are the true subjects of the historical project for social transformation. It is this belief that makes us think in the most radical and fundamental terms. Where there is weakness of this faith or belief, there is always room for dictatorship and monopoly and excuse for the lack of democracy of the people.

In our Asian history there have been many people's movements, although these have been suppressed by the ruling regimes and dismissed as riots and rebellions. Yet we must recognize the historical place of such people's movements and perceive their true nature, no matter how incomplete their struggles may have been. We must not again make the mistake of believing the official explanation about these movements. One can discern, invariably, a powerful people's language and wisdom without which they could not have launched their movement, even though they were subsequently suppressed because of their powerlessness. The T'aip'ing Rebellion and May Fourth Movement in China have been decisive parables for Chinese revolutionaries — although one cannot say categorically that all Chinese revolutionaries were faithful to the historical aspirations of the Chinese people. We must not neglect the parable of the people's movement if we take seriously the people as subjects of history.

At the same time we must give closer attention to the development of people's movements in Asia in order to discern the historical direction of the people. In fact, if we believe in the people, we must seek to catalyze and participate in their movements. Because of their powerlessness, these movements are often suppressed by military and police power; but in the process of movement, the people begin to discover their own words and their historical subjectivity, which are subversive of the technocratic and ideological language.

The Power of the People

Building the power of the people is essential to translate their historical subjectivity and their aspirations into historical reality and to counter the power of technocratic and other repressive regimes. Choosing the process by which to build the people's power is a most difficult task, but through long and arduous experiences, certain insights can be gained and new experiments tried. Several things are clear from past experience. People's power rises from the grassroots rather than being organized from the top. People's power is organized horizontally and is highly decentralized, not vertical and concentrated. People's power is often elusive and discreet under existing political conditions, and because of its relative weakness, it is precarious and easily co-opted. People's power may not have a permanent base geographically, but it can exist among the people wherever they are.

The stories of the people are told in terms of their suffering and their mastery over their own language, their own bodies, and their own future. To tell one's own story is to be in charge of one's own language, one's own body, and, therefore, one's own destiny. So in the act of telling their story, the people have already begun to exercise power. It is important, therefore, that people speak and tell their story. This is one way we can begin to speak about and deal with transnational corporations and the suffering they have caused. As we work out how to tell the story more loudly, more penetratingly, and in more moving and persuasive ways, we can deal concretely with the transnational corporations.

A second resource is somatic strength, bodily strength. I do not mean force, though of course force is important, but the bodily strength we feel when we experience history as a community or as a human body. Certain dynamics emerge in our bodies because of our perception and experience. In other words, we have to move; we cannot sit down all the time. This is fundamental. It is not just a physical movement; it is a bodily movement, but it is a movement of action, an act. We can say it is a form of historical praxis. Community organization may be an example of a bodily act. Politics by the people, of the people, is a bodily act.

Third, I want to talk about social imagination and give one example. In Korea, the March First Independence Movement of 1919 is regarded as the pivotal experience in Korean history, and a study of this movement shows that many people — ordinary people — participated, even though they were not really very well organized in modern political terms. We could say that they just acted spontaneously. Many social scientists and organizers believe this kind of spontaneous act is not useful in political struggles, which they feel must be tightly organized and controlled. But I must say this: the language that emerged at that time was very clearly a kind of indigenous apocalyptic language. The people were feeling apathetic and dispossessed; they were discouraged and were not acting. But somehow this apocalyptic language got into their bodies and they suddenly became militant, they suddenly changed. This phenomenon is very difficult to explain. The resources of social imagination in apocalyptic language — the belief that the whole old world is going to fall and a new world is going to come to be — give tremendous power.

Fourth, I mention the spiritual strength of the people and the mobilization of religious faiths in Asia. I think this aspect of our concern, even in Christian discussions, is much neglected and sometimes underplayed or distorted. *The story of the people is a spiritual drama.* Some social scientists define the well-being of the people only in terms of the calories that make one physically healthy, or the goods that satisfy one's material needs; this is a very cheap view of human development. The story of the people contains a rich life of spiritual struggle and meaning. The spiritual strength of the people, in particular, is the very power that makes them survive and struggle for tomorrow. Therefore, the mobilization of our religious strength is most important in terms of the resources of the people to deal with and fight the power of the transnational corporations.

Finally, what I call the *koinonia* of the people is our abiding resource. We talk about the solidarity of the people, but I would rather use the term *koinonia* because it refers to a concrete experience of the people. I think that even a brief time of being together gives us tremendous resources and generation of energy. It is difficult to define precisely. But among the people, this *koinonia* is a very important resource and power to deal with many different situations. Just to give you one example: how to deal with defeat in a concrete situation is very important in our struggles. We do not always have victories. So *koinonia* is an important resource that enables us to deal with defeat, to deal with not being able to understand, or to deal with the sense of powerlessness. *Koinonia* has the aspects of participation and sharing. The people's language and bodies, their role as gardeners, and their spirit form a sort of paradoxical power of the powerless. This is qualitatively different from the arbitrary, brute force of the ruling power; it is the power of truth, love, peace, and justice. It is the power of resistance against injustice. It is the power of brotherhood and solidarity of the people, full of human love. The power of the people emerges when they have the solidarity of *koinonia* among themselves. Their power is also their vision of their destiny; when the people move for tomorrow, their power rises.

This kind of people's power not only counterbalances brute force, but also challenges the nature and legitimacy of corporate power such as that of the transnational corporation. The reality of the people's power has some disturbing effects because there is no structural continuity between the power of the people and the power of the powerful. The former exposes the irrationality and injustice of the latter, thus beginning the transformation of the power of the giant corpus. The true human story of the people can then be created, which may be called the activity of humanization by the people.

Victory in the story of the people is not inherent, for no power can be organized successfully against giant corporate power on its own terms. Victory is an impossibility. Therefore, the story of the suffering people has to be connected with the story of the victorious historical miracle. Historical transformation is not wrought as the inherent logic of history, but the suffering of the people brings about such transformation as the *ultimum novum* (new tomorrow).

MINJUNG ECONOMICS: A NEW CONCEPT OF JUSTICE

Economics of the people is a science to secure the basic and whole life of the *minjung*. Land, resources, production, and distribution are arranged to secure the life of the people in its fullness and wholeness. No wealth or possession can be justified as right if it does not serve to secure the life of the people. No one has a right to property and wealth when the life of the people is not secured. This is the meaning of *minjung* economics. Here the question is not merely equal distribution, but the transformation of an economic system and order that deny the security of life of the *minjung*.

The crucial problem is that neither the capitalist system nor the socialist system has been able to create socio-economic conditions in which the security of life of the *minjung* is guaranteed. Rather they have denied the life of the *minjung*. They have served the monopoly of greed of the corporate powers and the hubris of the empires. The *minjung* must be freed from these imperial greeds.

The existing systems serve only a powerful minority of the world's people. The present economic systems see accumulation and growth as the primary means of staving off unemployment. Market mechanisms are assumed to be the most efficient method of resource exchange; they are regarded as best to solve whatever problems arise within the framework of this institution. It is assumed that economic agents behave rationally in the pursuit of their individual and institutional interests, and that this activity results in the achievement of the greatest good for the greatest number of people. It is assumed that consumer demand depends on consumer sovereignty and is motivated by the satisfaction of independently determined individual wants.

As in the socialist model, it is believed that the state is so good and wise that its planning, production, and distribution will accomplish economic justice and well-being. But this alternative paradigm of collective ownership and state control has not in fact overcome the greed of the powers or secured the life of the people. The body of the people, as individuals or as community, has not found the wholeness of life envisioned in their covenant with God. The state overrides the people's rights, both political and socio-economic.

The prevailing paradigms make particular assumptions about the relationship between humanity and nature, conceiving it unidirectionally as one of domination and utilization. The new paradigm will have to be based on a more reciprocal understanding of that relationship, with more respect and care for nature.[23]

Minjung Economics

Minjung economics (*oikonomia*) must fully secure the life of the *minjung*, as God has willed in God's own household. The *minjung's* well-being is grounded in God's justice and fulfilled in God's *shalom*. Their physical and socio-economic security is an integral part of their total well-being. The covenant of God with the poor is to secure their life that they may multiply and prosper.

But the political economy of the powerful has excluded the *minjung* from the life of *shalom* in various degrees and ways. The *minjung* are made poor by the system of the dominant political economy. The dominant economic organization of private corporations and the hegemony of state economies have alienated the *minjung* from their right to a secure life and chained them to poverty and oppression.

It is often stated that the church cannot identify with any particular economic system. This position is not tenable today, when the political economy of the imperial powers threatens the life of the people. The people should be free from enslavement to the existing world economic order. They need a concrete form of political economy in which their full and whole life is secured. The Christian faith must take concrete form through action and manifestation of itself in the reality of the political economy; that is, our faith must be a definite realization of the covenant with God.

The rights of workers are more than the right to organize, the right of collective bargaining, and the right to strike. Their fundamental right is to secure a full and whole life, through the establishment of a political economy as the framework of this life.

No equal distribution or division of property will suffice; the priority is the meeting of the needs of the poor for the wholeness of life of the people. When the socio-economic security of the whole community is secured, there will be no needy.

The story of the garden in Genesis 1 and 2 reveals the political economy of the sovereignty of God. God has created and entrusted the resources of the earth to humans, who are to cultivate *shalom*, to secure and safeguard life. The production and distribution of economic resources should be seen in this light. Production should be understood as gardening and distribution as sharing (*koinonia*). God has created the world and human beings as a garden.

Economic resources are God's gifts; this means that no person (individual or legal) may monopolize possession or deny others' fundamental needs and rights for a secure human life, as God has created and preserved and promised. This theological foundation does not allow the absolutization of private ownership or collective ownership by the state. The earth is the Lord's and the fullness thereof, the world and who they dwell therein (Ps. 24:1).

Economic activity — that is, work — is (1) a necessary condition for full and whole human life. Physical needs are met (food, shelter, clothing, and health) and spiritual needs are satisfied (education, creativity, and cultural life). Work is (2) a life of love and service under the sovereignty of God. It is a practical expression of love for one's neighbor. Work is (3) an activity to realize the self and community through the exercise of creative power. And work is (4) the tending of the garden of *shalom* in community and in nature. It is the gardening of full and whole human life and the fulfillment of the covenant with God. In short, work is participation in the political economy of God to create, protect, and fulfill the life and *shalom* of the people.

Economic justice is to protect the workers and the poor so that they do have the fullness of life and so that the wealthy do not misuse the resources that have been provided by God. Protection of the poor and guarantee of the rights of the workers are for their wholeness of life.

Jesus the friend of the poor is the originator of the social transformation and community life that characterized the early church; he protected the destitute, the weak, and the needy, and they had fellowship with him and with each other in a foretaste of the reign of God. It is the eschatological right of the poor to secure life as God has intended and promised.

The economy of the early Christian community in Acts 2:42–45 and 4:32–35 manifests God's political economy vividly:

> The whole group of believers was united, heart and soul; no one claimed for his own use anything that he had, as everything they owned was held in common.... None of their members was ever in want, as all those who owned land or houses would sell them, and bringing the money from them, would present it to the apostles; it was then distributed to any members who might be in need.

The *koinonia* described in the above was possible because the decisive lordship of Christ over their total life was realized through the Holy Spirit. And there were no poor among them.

Economics according to James meant respect for the poor, as in James 2:1–9:

> My brothers, do not try to combine faith in Jesus Christ, our glorified Lord, with the making of distinctions between classes of people.... It is those who are poor according to the world that God chose, to be rich in faith and to be heirs of the kingdom which he promised to those who love him.... Well, the right thing to do is to keep the supreme law of scripture: you must love your neighbor as yourself, but as soon as you make distinctions between classes of people, you are committing sin and under condemnation for breaking the Law.

A warning to the rich is part of the political economy of the early church as it is expressed in James 5:1–6:

> Now an answer for the rich. Start crying, weep for the miseries that are coming to you. Your wealth is all rotting, you clothes are eaten up by moths. All your gold and silver are corroding away, and the same corrosion will be your sentence, and eat into your body. It was a burning fire that you stored up as your treasure for the last days.

Laborers mowed your fields, and you cheated them — listen to the wages that you kept back, calling out; realize that the cries of the reapers have reached the ears of the Lord of hosts. On earth you have had a life of comfort and luxury; in the time of slaughter you went on eating to your heart's content. It was you who condemned the innocent and killed them; they offered you no resistance.

The political economy of New Jerusalem is made known in Revelation 21:1–4; 22:1–2:

Then I saw a new heaven and a new earth. I saw...the New Jerusalem....Here God lives among men. He will make his home among them; they shall be his people, and he will be their God; his name is God-with-them. He will wipe away all tears from their eyes; there will be no more death, and no more mourning or sadness.

Then the angel showed me the river of life...flowing crystal-clear down the middle of the city street. On either side of the river were the trees of life, which bear twelve crops of fruit in a year, one each month, and leaves of which are the cure for the pagans. Nations will come, bringing their treasure and wealth.[24]

Minjung Experiences: Socio-economic Wisdom of the People

In the context of the Asian civilizations we can find various religious and cultural resources to help us tend the garden of *shalom* — resources that have been developing through the people's movements. The Confucian vision of great peace and prosperity was appropriated by the people's struggles to overcome the powerful domination of the Confucian autocracy and foreign colonial power. An example of this is the peasant movement of T'aip'ing in nineteenth-century China. Another example is found in the Silhak (Realist) school of Korean Confucianism.

Another religious resource is the Buddhist school that envisions a Western Paradise, or Pure Land for the suffering people, where there is a harmonious wholeness of all the living and all suffering is ended. The Buddhist tradition depicts the present as a sea of suffering rising out of greed, a cousin of the institutionalized greed of profit maximization. Particularly the school of Maitreya Buddha has provided powerful religious and spiritual inspiration for the poor and oppressed, for this Buddha is the friend of the common people. Many of the people's movements in Asia have been related to this school of Buddhist thought.

Then there is the Taoist tradition, which recognizes perfect harmony between the human, the natural, and the supernatural. The Tao, which is the pervasive way of all the universe, is the principle of natural, not artificial, harmony. The Taoist vision of the world is truly that of the perfect garden, in which human beings live with longevity, like angelic beings. Therefore, the world is a garden of angels. As the Taoist sees it, the present world is an arbitrary and artificial reality in which humans struggle against each other. The Taoist teachings are particularly influential among the common people, sometimes becoming mixed up with popular beliefs like shamanism and animism.

There are other religious and spiritual traditions in Asia that hold a vision of the future as justice and peace. Here we cannot enumerate them all. But it is clear that the Asian peoples have rich religious and cultural resources that have been nurtured in the midst of their long sufferings.

The Buddhist concept of *sanga* (community) has been a source of inspiration for a social order in which human greed is checked and overcome. This can be a basis for the political economy of people who have the Buddhist faith. Buddhism is originally a *minjung* religion, in spite of the historical fact that it has been appropriated by the ruling regimes of many Asian countries. Buddhism reflects many of the *minjung* economic aspirations.

E. F. Schumacher's book *Small Is Beautiful* is not only a critical analysis of the present economic order, but also a socio-economic paradigm inspired by the religious faith of the people. As a modern economist, Schumacher takes an imaginative look into Buddhist economics. He observes, "'Right Livelihood' is one of the requirements of the Buddha's Noble Eightfold Path. It is clear, therefore, that there must be such a thing as Buddhist economics." For example, the Buddhist point of view takes the function of work to be at least threefold: to give us a chance to utilize and develop our faculties; to enable us to overcome our ego-centeredness by joining with other people in a common task; and to bring forth the goods and services needed for existence. Thus, Buddhist economics can realize such truths as simplicity and nonviolence in concrete theories for the economic life of the people.[25]

Kyongje or *kyongse chemin* (political economy of the people), which is "economy" in English, means "saving the people." There is another Korean term, *minsaeng*, which means "life of the people." Here *min*, which means "the people," has its origin in the term "slave." The *min* are the cultivators of the land; the land is owned by the king, and land reform is a major enterprise of the king to secure the life of the people who are enslaved to the aristocratic class and landlords. The virtuous king rules to secure the life of the people; and the heart of the *min* is the heart of heaven (*minsim ch'onsim*).

The Confucian ideal of the Prosperous Age of the Great Peace (*T'aip'ing*) manifested itself in the popular tradition of Confucianism as well as in the ruling ideology of the Confucian dynasties. One outstanding modern example is the T'aip'ing Peasant Movement with its land reforms.

In Korea we find one of the finest examples of Confucian land reform in the Realist School of Korean Confucianism. A Korean Confucian scholar, Chong Yak-yong (1762–1836), advocated the *yojon* land system, that is, community ownership, community production, and common sharing. Thirty households would own an appropriate amount of land, and the whole community would cooperatively carry out production and share the harvest according to the needs of the people, for the security of the whole community. Unfortunately, this reform could never be carried out, for there was no political backing for it.[26]

Chong Yak-yong's Confucian reform is an example of the political economy of Confucian rule in a particular social and historical situation. This is instructive for the Christian faith, because of its implication that a Christian political economy could be worked out in a particular historical context.

Economics of the People

In the tradition of the people a popular economics has developed as a part of the crystallization of the people's wisdom. In Korea a system of *kye* was developed, a cooperative system to alleviate major financial burdens cooperatively among the *kye* members. *Ture* is another such plan, in which the members share the work to be done in a cooperative manner in order to overcome labor problems and shortages. Such popular economic wisdom has never been taken seriously by the prevailing economic forces, which benefit from the existing political economy. But such popular economic wisdom can be developed into a viable political economy. At least we need to take seriously the basic wisdom of the people for our elaboration of political economic thinking. Current economic theories claim universal validity, but they represent the dominant economic system; the people's economic aspirations are not directly reflected.

The fundamental point here is that the political economy of the sovereignty of God in biblical history should and can be the real foundation upon which the people of God live out their faith in contemporary economic life.

Examination of economic life in the light of biblical faith has, most often, taken the form of a simple reiteration of certain aspects of the economic teachings that are spelled out in the New Testament, especially certain teachings of Jesus that have direct reference to the acquisition, possession, and use of material goods. The sharpest and most demanding of these are frequently dismissed as eschatological sayings or as hyperboles. Structural and institutional manifestation of the faith in economic life has been ignored, and economic ethics has taken the form of a highly individualistic morality.

Stewardship is the responsibility before God and the people to secure the full and whole life of the people. Talent is to be used to secure both one's own full life and to serve God by serving the people for their full and whole life. The concept of vocation, that is, glorifying God through one's calling, has brought about diligence in work and thrift in expenditures, but originally it meant dedication of one's work and possessions to the glory of God and the service of one's neighbors.

Private property is defined by the class that uses it. The meaning of property has changed continuously, according to changes in the purpose that the dominant classes expect the institution of property to serve.

The various definitions of property clearly have served the wealthy and powerful. The sovereignty of God over property liberates property to be defined as the basis of security of the whole community. In the context of the covenant of God and the people of God, property and its definition cannot serve the rich and powerful, for that would justify the greed of the political and economic powers and thereby threaten the full and secure life of the people. This challenges any absolutist or ideological concept of property that justifies power, whether socialist or capitalist. It opens the door to concrete definitions of property that see property as the realization of security for the whole life of the people.

Economic justice is not merely the undoing of injustice and exploitation. It is the liberation of the slaves and the protection of the poor and others who are robbed of their economic means to enjoy a full and whole life. Economic justice is more than economic production, economic growth, equal distribution, and a socio-economic welfare system. It is the political economy of the people, whose life is fully and wholly secured and enjoyed.

The fundamental needs of the poor neighbor should be met; but these needs are to be secured as God has promised, and therefore the neighbor's needs are not merely needs, but his or her *rights*. To allow a situation to continue whereby needs are not met is a violation of these rights and thereby the violation of God's will.

When the church can take form as a genuine community that transcends social and class lines, it makes one of its most important contributions to the resolution of economic problems and conflicts in society.

The political economy of the household is that of sharing, whereas the political economy of corporate capitalism and state capitalism in its international and national forms is that of profit maximization and domination by power.

The Christian churches have not taken this position very seriously, due mainly to their conformity to the capitalist world. Now is the time when the reality of the political economy of the sovereignty of God must find its expression in the concrete socio-economic life of the peoples of the world, especially those of the Third World.

Christian Community as the Gardener for a Full and Whole Life of Justice and Shalom

Christian community as an ecumenical movement for justice, peace, and integrity of creation is a movement to cultivate justice, *koinonia*, and *shalom* in the universe. In this context we recognize that the subject of the gardening work is the people of God, and at the same time that all created things, not merely humans, are participants in the garden. The sin of the Leviathan and Dinosaur has been to make not only all humans but all created things the objects of exploitation and oppression, and this sin has turned God's created garden into a jungle.

This theological perspective has profound implications for the correction of the scientific epistemology that tends to regard itself as an objective and objectifying process, although nowadays there are some efforts to correct this situation among scientists and philosophers of science. Perhaps the analytical method needs to be corrected, that is, its tendency to generalize limited hypotheses beyond their proper scope. Such fallacies distort the integrated whole of experience in which the created order, human and natural, is involved as active, participating agents in the drama of God's gardening.

Technocracy should be conceived anew as creative work to cultivate justice, *koinonia*, and *shalom* in the universe, as God has created it and continues to create it. It should not be an instrument for simple profit maximization or survival of the mightiest. Perhaps this requires a radical reorganization of the human community in which science and technology become agents to garden the universe.

In the light of the biblical vision of the garden of justice, *shalom*, and harmony (integrity) of creation, these religious and cultural resources, particularly those appropriated by the poor and oppressed, can be revitalized to become the flowers, fruits, and even roots of various elements in the garden of God, in which humans are also gardeners.

The garden has been turned into the jungle. Now the Dinosaur and Leviathan have to be subjugated to God the gardener, the injured human community and natural order have to be healed and revitalized, and the Spirit of life must fill the world so that there may be true justice, *koinonia*, and *shalom* in the garden. This is the task of the people of God in God's *oikoumene*, which is God's dwelling among the people of the created world.

In this garden the leopard is replaced by the shepherd, the master is replaced by the servant, and the Leviathan is replaced by the Lamb, who is the sacrificial Lord. In this way the oppressive political order, unjust exploitation, war for security and survival, and destruction of nature will be expelled from the created order of God, and justice, peace, and integrity of creation will be fulfilled in the garden.

The covenant with the poor thus guarantees the *shalom* of the human community, genuine community based on justice and *agape*. This is the manifestation of the sovereignty of God. Faith in God is the source of freedom from the self-centeredness of hubris and power and the source of freedom for the covenant. This faith is expressed in a social imagination that seeks actualization through social theories and in social experiments that practice the radical freedom of faith in the fulfillment of the covenant with the *minjung*.

Notes

1. The notion of political economy is used here to refer to God's rule over the political and economic life of the people of God. The Korean term *kyongse chemin* has precisely this meaning of political economy.

2. The Universal Christian Conference on Life and Work,

Stockholm, 1925, treated economic life in the framework of the gospel as being for all realms of life.

3. See C. B. MacPherson, *Property* (Oxford: Basil Blackwell, 1978), a history of economic theories since Adam Smith that describes the development of the autonomy of economics.

4. Charles West, Harvey Cox, Lynn White, and Friedrich Gogarten are some who advocate the secularization thesis in historical and theological terms.

5. The giant transnational corporations and state economic systems are prime examples. They have justified their own existence in ideological terms. This economic power can be linked to the biblical notion of Mammon.

6. The notion of "corporate responsibility" has been applied to criticize and pressure the misconduct of the multinational corporations. For example, the role of these corporations in South Africa has been widely questioned by the churches.

7. See Max Weber, *Protestant Ethics and the Spirit of Capitalism* and Richard H. Tawney, *The Rise of Capitalism*.

8. Peter d'A. Jones, *Christian Socialist Revival* (Princeton, N.J.: Princeton University Press, 1968). See also the ecumenical statement of the WCC Amsterdam Assembly on economic and political organization, in *Statements of the World Council of Churches on Social Questions* (Geneva, 1956), 18ff.

9. John C. Bennett, *Christianity and Our World* (New York, 1936), 33ff.

10. Richard J. Barnet and Ronald E. Muller, *Global Reach: the Power of Multinational Corporations* (New York: Simon and Schuster, 1974).

11. John K. Galbraith, *New Industrial State* (New York: Mentor, 1979).

12. See the study by the World Council of Churches, Commission on Participation in Development, *Transnational Corporations, Technology and Human Development*, 1980.

13. See *Ecumenical Reflections on Political Economy* (Geneva: WCC-CCPD, 1988).

14. Clinton Gardner, *Biblical Faith and Social Ethics* (New York: Harper and Brothers, 1960), 287.

15. Andre Bieler, "Gradual Awareness of Social and Economic Problems (1750–1899)," in Julio de Santa Ana, ed., *Separation without Hope* (Geneva: CCPD-WCC, 1978).

16. See Charles C. West, *Communism and Theologians* (Philadelphia: Westminster Press, 1958), 78–104, 128–39, 181–89.

17. Gardner, *Biblical Faith and Social Ethics*, 286.

18. The World Conference on Church, Community and State, held in Oxford in 1937, pointed out problems in the capitalist economic system in the context of the Depression, but these criticisms were meant to modify the capitalist system.

19. A very good review of the ecumenical debate on economic questions has been done by Rob van Drimmelen in *Transformation*, June–December 1987.

20. An excellent and succinct description of Pax Romana is found in Klaus Wengst, *Pax Romana and the Peace of Jesus Christ* (London: SCM Press, 1987).

21. See the following:
1 Kings 17:1–18:46: Political economy of Baal versus that of Elijah
1 Kings 21:1–29: Naboth's vineyard

22. See the following:
1 Kings 3:22–28: Details of Solomon's horse-trading operation
1 Kings 6:1–38: The building of the temple
1 Kings 7:1–51: Solomon's building operations
1 Kings 11:1–8: Political economy of the foreign gods
1 Kings 11:9–13: Broken covenant in Solomon's reign

23. CCPD, *Ecumenism and New World Order: The Failure of the 70s and the Challenges of the 80s* (Geneva: CCPD, 1980), 17.

24. Additional biblical references are as follows:
Economy of Manna (Exod. 16:1–36): "At twilight you shall eat flesh, and in the morning you shall be filled with bread: then you shall know that I am the Lord.... This is what the Lord has commanded: 'Gather of it, every man of you, as much as he can eat; you shall take ... according to the number of persons whom each of you has in his tent.' They gathered, some more and some less. But when they measured it with omer, he that gathered much had nothing left over, and he that gathered little had no lack; *each gathered according to what he could eat*" (emphasis added).
Political Economy of the Covenant Code (Exod. 20:22–23:33): The right of the slave: "When you buy a Hebrew slave, he shall serve six years, and in the seventh he shall go free, for nothing" (Exod. 21:2, Deut. 15:12-18).

Rights of the female slave: Exodus 21:7–11
Laws protecting human life: Exodus 21:12–32
Laws dealing with property: Exodus 21:33–22:17
You shall not steal: Exodus 20:15
Social rights of the weak: Exodus 22:21–27; 23:9
Sabbath of the land and animals: Exodus 23:10–12
Economy of feasts before the Lord: Exodus 23:14–19
Political economy of Sabbatical year and Jubilee (Lev. 25): The land shall keep the Sabbath. The ownership of the land is vested in God, not human beings.

"It shall be a year of solemn rest for the land. The Sabbath of the land shall provide food for you, for yourself and for your male and female slaves and for your hired servant and the sojourner who lives with you; for your cattle also and for the beasts that are in your land all its yield shall be for food" (Lev. 25:5–7).

"And you shall hallow the fiftieth year, and proclaim liberty throughout the land to all inhabitants; it shall be a jubilee for you, when each of you shall return to his property and each of you shall return to his family...so you will dwell in the land securely. The land will yield its fruit, and you will eat your fill, and dwell in it securely. The land shall not be sold in perpetuity, for the land is mine; for you are strangers and sojourners with me. In all the country you possess, you shall grant a redemption of the land."

Sociology of census in Numbers: "the house of his fathers," that is, the tribe.

Allotment of the land: Numbers 32:1–42; 34:1–29.

Inheritance law (Num. 36:1–12): Intertribal land transfer is prohibited. "So no inheritance shall be transferred from one tribe to another; for each of the tribes of the people of Israel shall cleave to his own inheritance" (Num. 36:9).

Political economy of Ten Commandments (Exod. 20 and Deut.): "I am the Lord your God, who brought you out of the land of Egypt, out of the house of bondage. You shall have no gods before me....Observe the Sabbath day....Neither shall you steal....Neither shall you covet your neighbor's wife; and you shall not desire your neighbor's house, his field, or his manservant or his maidservant, his ox, or his ass, or anything that is your neighbor's."

God has promised a land flowing with milk and honey to the people of God; and promised a "land with great and goodly cities...and houses full of all good things...and cisterns hewn out, vineyards and olive trees" (Deut. 6:10–15). This is the promise behind the first commandment.

This promise of socio-economic security is assured and promised by God; and it means that the political economy of the city kingdoms of Canaan must be rejected altogether with its religious undergirdings (Deut. 7:1–11; 7:12–16; 8:1–10): "You shall not make covenant with them."

Deuteronomy 15: Liberation of the political economy at the end of the seventh year. Also Deuteronomy 14:28–29: "At the end of every three years you shall bring forth all the tithe of your produce in the same year, and lay it up within your town; and the Levite, because he has no portion or inheritance with you, and the sojourners, the fatherless, and the widow, who are within your towns, shall come and eat and be filled; that the Lord your God may bless you in all the work you do."

"Justice, and only justice, you shall follow, that you may live and inherit the land which the Lord your God gives you" (Deut. 16:20).

This also means that property is the gift and blessing of God to secure the life of the people. Particularly, it is to protect the poor, that is, the Hebrew slaves. This also means strict prevention of self-centeredness in economic life. It became the basis of economic servanthood, which has traditionally been called stewardship.

Rich Christians (1 Tim. 6:17–19): "Warn those who are rich in this world's goods that they are not to look down on other people; and not to set their hopes on money, which is untrustworthy, but on God, who, out of his riches, gives us all that we need for our happiness. Tell them that they are to do good, and be rich in good works, to be generous and willing to share — this is the way they can save up a good capital sum for the future if they want to make sure of the only life that is real."

Paul's teaching to the Corinthians (2 Cor. 8, 9): "Remember how generous the Lord Jesus was: 'He was rich, but he became poor for your sake, to make you rich out of poverty....As long as readiness is there, a man is acceptable with whatever he can afford; never mind what is beyond his means.' This does not mean that to give relief to others you ought to make things difficult for yourselves; it is a question of balancing what happens to be your surplus now against their present need, and one day they may have something to share that will supply your own need. This is how we strike a balance; as scripture says: 'The man who gathered much had none too much, the man who gathered little did not go short.' "

25. E. F. Schumacher, *Small Is Beautiful* (London: Harper and Row, 1975), 53–62.

26. Shin Yong Ha, "The Idea of Yojonje Land Reform System by Chong Tasan (Chong Tasaneui Yojonje Tojikaehyuk Sasang)" in Han U Keun et al., *Present State of the Study on Chong Tasan (Chong Tasan Yonkueui Hyonghwang)* (Seoul: Mineumsa, 1985), 192–217.

4

RECLAIMING A THEOLOGY OF POWER FROM THE GOSPEL MIRACLE STORYTELLERS

Antoinette Clark Wire

I must begin by recognizing the difficulty of what I want to do. Internationally the United States is known in our time for claims to power beyond its own borders, both economic and political, and a North American speaking today about a theology of power is in danger of being heard as if she were speaking imperially. This is a severe risk. But I cannot speak as a Christian woman today without talking about power. If pride and thirst for power are the besetting sins of the male of our species, the female is as severely tempted to fear and dependence and must learn responsible participation in power. What does it mean today that the gospel is the power of God for salvation, that is, for making all people well and whole and responsible?

There is one part of the gospel tradition in which power plays a major role: the stories about miraculous acts of Jesus. Perhaps for this reason we hear very little about these stories, or we hear them simply as stories about Jesus helping people. But even a quick second look shows us they claim to tell about events of power. It is not Jesus who tells the stories about others, but others are telling about Jesus. So the stories do not claim to represent his viewpoint, as do his parables and other teachings, and in a number of cases they are told in spite of the fact that Jesus tells someone not to tell the story.

Those who study the origin and development of the gospels think they were written not by Jesus' disciples but by second-generation Christians from material about Jesus that had been handed down orally for thirty to seventy years before being written as gospels. Apparently, different groups of people handed down different stories. One theory is that Christian prophets kept preaching Jesus' warnings and announcements of God's reign from town to town, while settled Christian communities told about Jesus' dying and rising as they celebrated together his last meal and baptized people into his death and new life.

But who were telling and retelling the miracle stories? If no one had kept telling them, the unwritten stories would have been forgotten and disappeared from history before any gospel was written. The best clues about these storytellers are in the stories themselves, since people do not tell a story repeatedly unless it expresses their interests, talks about their kind of people, or reflects their assumptions. The assumptions reflected here were shared by almost all people in the Mediterranean world of that time, assumptions about unclean spirits taking up residence in people, about sickness being caused by sin and healed by the prayer or touch of a divinely sent person. The kind of people in these stories is a narrower group — small-town or rural Galilean people with massive physical needs. Finally, the interests expressed in the stories further specify who among all the hard-pressed peasants the tellers were. These interests can be determined only by reviewing the structure of the stories. Though each successive teller or writer of a single story tells it somewhat differently, this does not change the story's most basic structure, which has three components: the underlying interaction or conflict, its intensification, and its final resolution. From my study of all the gospel miracle stories I have come up with four major types of story structure, showing the four major interests of the people who kept on telling these stories.

STORY TYPES

The first story type I call the *exorcism*. Here the struggle is between a nonhuman power on the one side, which has taken over a person and threatens to destroy or annihilate him or her, and, on the other side, a stranger newly arrived on the scene whose presence puts this power on the defensive. You will recognize here Mark's story of the unclean spirit in Capernaum (1:21–28), the Gadarene demoniac (5:1–20), the boy with seizures (9:14–21), and, if you look twice, also the boat full of disciples on the stormy lake (4:35–41). The other gospels except John tell parallel stories. There are also similar stories about expelled plagues and vampires in other ancient literature.[1] The tension is intensified by the engagement of the two forces, the evil power often reacting first by shouting adjurations and insults or by exposing the stranger's name, the other holding ground and calmly asking the evil power questions about itself. The resolution comes when the stranger struggles with and expels the destroying force, which may convulse the one possessed before it leaves and then destroy some nonhuman object to demonstrate its own destruction.

The once-possessed persons or boatload of persons have no active role in these stories. But these endangered people provide the point of identification for the storyteller and hearer and show what their interest is in telling the story, namely, to celebrate the rescue of someone like themselves from sure death and his or her restoration to life. We cannot tell exactly what kind of life-threatening situation makes the storyteller and hearer so interested in retelling this kind of story — whether they fear destruction by madness or death at sea, or the military "legions" of Rome suggested by one of the unclean spirits' names. In our time there are also life-threatening powers, such as cancer and nuclear war, that make us interested in these stories. When people's own lives are on the line, then it really means something to tell how these people who had lost control even of their own voices and limbs to annihilating powers were nonetheless rescued and restored to a secure life.

Another group of stories turns on conflict between religious authorities and Jesus concerning right and wrong conduct. The authorities construe the law strictly to protect God from the people — God's day, God's forgiveness, God's temple must be inviolate — whereas their opponent breaks through the law's restrictions with a miracle on behalf of a person in need (Mark 2:1–12; 3:1–6; Matt. 12:22–30 and parallels; Luke 13:10–17; 14:1–6; Matt. 17:24–27). It is important to note that this is not a conflict between two religions; both Jesus and the authorities are Jews, and Jesus is not the only Jew in this period known for use of miracle power against standard legal interpretations. There is a wonderful story about Rabbi Eliezer, who is said to make a stream flow backward to prove that a certain oven is clean.[2] This story type I call the *exposé*, because a rural rabbi like Jesus exposes the educated rabbis who interpret the law strictly in order to defend their own reputations rather than God, who needs no protection from the people. In our world it is academic and political as well as religious authorities who make themselves the measure of right and wrong. Jesus exposes the authorities by asking a single question about politics, or treatment of farm animals, or which of two things is better or easier — for example, "Is it allowed on the sabbath to save a life or to kill?" (Mark 3:4) — and this exposes the absurdity of restrictive laws. The power of this truth is then demonstrated in a miraculous event that sets the restricted person free.

These stories deal not with evil that annihilates but with the kind of moral evil that calls the common people violators of God so that the authorities look like God's protectors. Yet the storyteller is, if anything, yet more strongly interested in exploding their credibility and power. There is no interest shown in reconstructing what might be a more proper religious observance, because the teller identifies not with the system but with the person caught in it — the woman bent double, the man with the withered hand — and tells the story to claim God's power to shame the system. The people who keep telling these stories for at least half a century may be continuing to struggle with a brand of Pharisaic Judaism, or they may be telling the stories against other religious and social systems. But they continue to use Jesus' commonsense questions to expose the class of people whose superiority is a fiction of their own construction, falsely making others inferior.

A third, very different kind of story concerns the *provision* of food or drink in the gospels, specifically fish (Luke 5:4–11; John 21:4–8), bread (Mark 6:30–44; 8:1–10 and parallels; John 6:1–14), and wine (John 2:1–11). By the time these stories are written in the gospels, the point has in many cases shifted from provision of food to the universal mission of the church in catching human beings or to the fellowship of the Lord's supper. But the constant structure of the stories shows that the early tellers were interested in the concrete problem of people who have run out of the staple food (which for the Jewish village wedding was wine). The tension is heightened when Jesus expects them nonetheless to carry out the tasks of provision — to let down the nets, seat the people and distribute, fill jars and pour glasses. And only when they do so in spite of themselves, then boats founder, baskets overflow, and wine is more and better than people can accept. In the earlier written and probably oral versions of each story (John 2:9; Mark 6:30–44; Luke 5:4–11) only those who do the work seem to know what has happened. In this way the teller gives the hearer an insider's position in the story and an interest in taking the risk of providing in spite of resignation or fear. Jesus' role remains indispensable as the one giving instructions, but it is no longer central to the action because the providers must ultimately "do their own miracle." Those interested in telling such stories are clearly wanting to challenge others to take courage and provide boldly as Jesus instructs.

The final type of gospel miracle story I call the *demand* story. Because the majority of gospel miracle stories fall in this category, it has been said that Jesus never does miracles in the gospels unless someone makes a demand on him. But in fact the victims in exorcism stories often have no voice of their own, in exposés are too afraid to use it, and in feedings are too resigned. As we have seen, it is Jesus who acts on behalf of the possessed and the marginalized, and he teaches people to be feeders. But in the demand stories the initiative begins and ends with the person demanding a healing; Jesus plays other, less central roles. In some stories he intensifies their demand by asking questions or rebuking their unfaith, saying, "Do you want to be well?" or "All things are possible to one who believes." Other demand stories are intensified by some physical obstruction that tests the person's demand. Blind Bartimaeus of Jericho has to out-shout the crowd around Jesus and defy all those trying to silence him before he gets Jesus' attention. The hemorrhaging woman must push her way through a mob to touch him. Jesus responds to these two by saying, "Your faith made you well," confirming the crucial role of their demand in their healing.

Or the demand may be intensified by some opposition of Jesus himself. Jesus refuses to heal the Syrophoenician woman's daughter (Mark 7:24–30) and says, "It is not right to throw the children's food to the dogs." But her retort steps right into his proverb, "Even the dogs eat the children's crumbs," and he cannot make a comeback except to concede, "On account of this word, go; the demon has gone out of your daughter." This perfect tense in Mark's telling — "the demon has gone out" — indicates that it is her word, her demand, which has brought healing for her daughter.

And Jesus intensifies the demand by his own opposition whenever he tries to prevent someone from telling the story of a healing.[3] After Jesus heals the dumb man by putting fingers into his ears and touching his tongue, he charges him to tell no one. In the gospels it is always the one who makes a demand who is told not to tell or who is described telling a story. This means that the story is understood to belong to the one who has gained what he or she pressed for. When this one tells the story over Jesus' opposition, the irrepressibility of this demand and its effect are evident. The story is shown to be not a neutral account but an assertion of an interest. Any storyteller who includes the silencing in the story becomes, so to speak, an accomplice in advocating the person's right to tell the

story. Most interesting is that no one hesitates to tell —
not the story character, the oral teller, the writer, or for
that matter myself today. The entire line of tradents is
convinced that the battle over the story between the one
who demanded the healing and the one who conceded it
should be resolved in favor of the demander whose story
we are hearing — that this only glorifies the healer. As
Mark says, the more he silenced them, the more they
proclaimed it.

As a whole, the demand stories demonstrate that the
storytellers side with and continue to tell the story of
the person who demanded to be well. Health is taken,
if you will, as a right that Jesus either actively encourages,
concedes with grace, or has no choice but to concede.

In all their four different kinds of story — exorcism,
exposé, provision, and demand — the tellers' stories celebrate the rural people's restoration to a basic humanity
not subject to threats of annihilation and humiliation. By
telling these stories they claim the power from God to feed
themselves and to realize their own demands for health
and wholeness.

MIRACLES AS PROBLEMATIC

Why have we heard so little in our churches and seminaries about these tellers and their important claims? I think
there are two major reasons. One reason we don't deal
with these stories is our offense at the miraculous as the
stories conceive it. In popular culture in both West and
East there has been a longstanding practice to distinguish
from normal events certain divine acts that are told as
"impossible" occurrences. Today our educational system
is built on the assumption that all mysterious aspects of
experience can eventually be understood within one somehow interrelated network of causality. Because the miracle
story genre was formulated by popular culture for report-
ing what is taken as at once actual and impossible,[4] it
simply doesn't fit scientific categories of thought. Educated
Christians who do not evade these stories tend to ignore

their miraculous elements, or they assume a special kind of causality for Sundays and holidays.

Far better that we recognize this problem and work at it seriously. Could we be something of a bridge between popular experience of truth and the scientists who test and codify truth in our cultures? On the one hand we need to determine how our religious tradition can contribute creatively to certain ways science perceives the universe. Science is unquestionably much more open to the place of mystery or indeterminate reality today than when most of us were educated. And people's stories unquestionably speak truth about God's empowering the poor, a truth that those whose education has made them consider themselves superior need to hear. On the other hand we can be open to scientific critique of popular assumptions in our tradition. If Jesus had problems with the miracle storytellers, we can expect to as well, especially where people retell other people's stories to monopolize power for themselves. Perhaps the everyday and the divine are not as far apart as the stories imply. We see God working here through human struggle, challenge, and demand. Yet we cannot ignore that the tellers chose to tell these reports as miracle stories. They insisted that the breakthrough they experienced in the radical evil that structured their lives came as no less than an act of God.

The second and I think equally important reason we have not heard these stories is the same reason they were considered subversive in the first place. These are the voice of the people in their own idiom, celebrating what they see to be an actual change in a person's physical and social life. The stories about this change affect other people who hear, and the power thus generated to claim a new physical and social life threatens to change the lives of comfortable people. We sense that the story makes us uncomfortable and our pastors kindly look for another text.

But at the same time I suggest we also hear in these stories a new hope. Is it an unreal hope, one only for the naive? Is it a revolutionary hope of the poor and a dangerous threat to the rest of us? Or could these peoples' stories form the basis for a theology of power that we could join the world's people in claiming? To answer these questions we need to know what kind of theology of power these stories celebrate and what it takes to join those who claim it.

MIRACLE STORIES AS THEOLOGY

In the first place, these stories celebrate a power that struggles against evil. Jesus takes on the unclean spirit that throws the helpless boy into the fire and then into the water in order to kill him. At the next turn Jesus takes on the religious authorities who prove themselves right at the expense of everyone else's being wrong. This is mental, moral, social, and physical evil, everything that violates people's humanity and prevents them from becoming the whole human beings that they are. It can be hunger that does it, or the isolation of leprosy, or a storm at sea, or taxes you can't pay, or the death of a child, or going crazy, or being treated as unclean, or even running out of wine at your daughter's wedding. Jesus confronts this evil directly and defeats it.

Within the stories there is no consistent personification of evil. These are not stories about warring gods or divine vengeance, but simply about something gone terribly wrong within a good creation where God wills life for all creatures. Lacking a simple explanation for evil, these stories also lack any social analysis or historical program for the struggle. But what they give is the most essential element, namely, the energy to enter the struggle for God's creation whenever life is obstructed in the confidence that God's power is present to overcome the evil that is violating that person.

Second, these stories challenge those affected by evil to claim the power to be human. The demoniac is told, "Go home to your own people and tell them," the man with the withered hand is charged, "Come out here in the center," and the paralytic is told, "Get up, lift your bed and walk" (Mark 5:19; 3:3; 2:9). Stronger challenges are found in the provision and demand stories. There *is* no miracle in the provision story if the group in question does not carry out the challenge to distribute the food, let down the nets, or pour the water as wine. And many of the demand stories begin rather weakly until the person is challenged, "Do not fear, only believe" (Mark 5:36). It certainly cannot be said that the tellers of these stories are waiting for manna from heaven or an external solution from above. Everything in the story turns on the persons involved taking responsibility, as if this were the issue in the first place, whether a whole person could be found here.

As well as celebrating the struggle against evil and the challenge to be whole, the demand stories in particular dramatize the irrepressible claim of the right to be well. In the face of all obstacles thrown up in the narrative — the distance, the disciple's weakness, the crowds, even the death of the one who needs healing — their demand gets stronger rather than weaker. Finally even the healer cannot hold out against them; they get what they need and tell their story to whom they will. Here the power is not being demonstrated by the healer's struggle or cultivated by his challenges but belongs to the protagonist from the opening demand to the final telling.

None of this struggle, challenge, or claim is seeking power to dominate others, to outdo others, or even to excel in any human skill or knowledge. Each demonstration of power is a demonstration of the power just to be human — to be alive and sane in the exorcism stories, to be treated decently as are farm animals in the exposé stories, to be able to feed oneself in the provision stories, to be well in the demand stories. If the power to be sane, respected, fed, and well sounds to us too basic or too low on the ladder of human achievement to be interesting, then we are not in a position to participate in the hope these stories offer. But if that power to be human is what we most want for ourselves as individuals and families and nations, then we can and will join the tellers in celebrating these stories.

You may wonder why I call this a *theology* of power, since the knowledge of God is not a dominant theme in these stories. But insofar as Jesus reveals who God is, these stories make a strong correction of so much Christian theology. They tell us God is not intent on God's own three persons or two natures or single sovereignty. In Jesus God is at work to restore the basic wholeness of human creatures by whatever method works — by frontal attack on powers that destroy and degrade people, by challenge to get people going, and most dramatically by giving way to people's boldness against all odds, even giving up best-laid divine plans for Israel's priority when a woman turns Jesus' rebuke to her advantage, and sensible plans for a long teaching ministry for Jesus when people have fantastic and dangerous stories to tell. God is above all the God of the people's power, the God of a reign that belongs to the poor and is entered by children. And these stories tell us that God likes it that way, the people like it that way, and when all is said and done, finding ourselves not one bit more than human, we like it that way too.

MODERN MIRACLES: A CHINESE CASE STUDY

Yet a major question remains. How can all this become reality today? Ours is a time when miracle stories sound archaic, when life moves very fast, and when God's marginal people are more likely to be found doing piecework for an unseen foreign company on a bad sewing machine. How do people recover their humanity under such conditions? Rather than talk in generalities or cite scattered examples, I would like to take up one broad test case in claiming divine power today. Last fall I had the great privilege of spending several months in China at Nanjing Union Theological Seminary, reading in journals of the 1950s and talking to people about the founding of the Chinese Christian Three-Self Movement and its biblical interpretation. Though I have more questions than answers, I can introduce something of their experience for our discussion.

The Chinese church was very small at the time of the revolution in 1949 — it is still less than 1 percent of the population, though the number of Christians has grown many times in the last ten years — and the church in 1949 was almost entirely financed and staffed at the top from abroad. The great struggle of the church in the years after the revolution concerned how to orient itself for survival and witness in a radically different world. Virtue seemed to call for stoic faithfulness to the past as their foreign friends and funding gradually were edged out and China's church made its isolated and suffering witness until the Lord came. Some devoted Christians maintained this stand and it may be that their pessimism about the world kept them from being coopted in the good times and disillusioned in the hard times to come.

But a few people, led by a remarkable lay YMCA secretary, Y. T. Wu, had a very different experience. Feeling, one of them has said, very much like Mary Magdalene weeping at the tomb and hoping at best to recover the remains of Christ, they like her were accosted by the living Christ calling them by name and saying, "Why are you crying?" They had to recognize that God was doing something completely new in their own time and they had become its witnesses.[5] While the church, in spite of its wealth, had had no appreciable effect in changing the gross injustices in society, they saw people who did not even believe in God doing just this. The revolutionaries had put a half-dead nation on the road to recovery after the Christians had played the priest and Levite, walking by on the other side of the road. This group of Christians suddenly saw they had been latter-day Pharisees, dutiful but self-righteous, busy locking those who did not share their traditions out of God's reign. So when other Christians argued that faith alone mattered in a godless world, they began to retort that faith without works was dead and that true faith was found not in words but in feeding the hungry and clothing the least. This "recovery of the gospel" was so convincing to them because they were sure that God, whether recognized or not, was at work in the national independence and land reform that was lifting up the hopes of the common people. From now on, they said, the church had to tell right from wrong, justice from oppression. This meant it had to repent and accept the whole world as the potential arena of God's activity.[6]

This repentance was not an academic question in postrevolutionary China and did not lead to any quick or easy experience of God's power. A group of church leaders went to Beijing in 1950 to make a complaint about local confiscation of church properties in violation of the government's freedom of religion policy. After three meetings with Premier Chou En Lai they decided that the problem could not be solved by a government decree but only by a new approach of the church to postrevolutionary China. The manifesto this group wrote, which was eventually signed by four hundred thousand Christians, admitted that the church had been used by foreign groups seeking to dominate China and resolved to become as quickly as possible completely self-governing, self-supporting, and self-propagating, criticizing itself wherever any sign of special privilege remained.[7] In the next years the church publicly denounced a number of foreign and Chinese Christian leaders who refused to make this kind of self-criticism. When some said that the church should not criticize foreigners after receiving so much from them, the answer again was taken from Scripture. Jesus ate in the Pharisees' homes and yet did not compromise the woes he announced against them.[8]

This experience of cleansing, though it was traumatic for some Christians, opened the church up to a new solidarity with the people of China and a new experience of power. As the church became an active part of the society working for changes, the gospel stories took on sharp contemporary meanings. The editors of the *Tian Feng* did a running series interpreting the gospel of Luke, including this statement on the hemorrhaging woman and the girl who dies while she is waiting to be healed.

Women in every social class are oppressed, even when the degree of oppression varies a little. Society oppresses women, though at times it likes to think that it shows them sympathy, that it treasures them, that it protects them in the cage of propriety, all until it suffocates and kills them. The woman, who in her bloody misery breaks through propriety and throws aside all caution, pushes through to the side of her liberating and saving Lord and becomes whole. The little girl with too narrow vision to break through propriety dies. How many weak women have been martyrs to propriety! The oppression is truly too great! But now the revolution has come. Even if she herself is not strong enough to break out of her confinement to seek liberation, the revolution's great tide will take the initiative to come to her. The Lord Jesus himself entered into the confined home and the little girl got up.[9]

Jesus' own solidarity with his people was taken as the Christian's prime example. He wept when he saw Jerusalem; the people escorted him into the city with palm branches; he threw the money-changers out of the nation's temple. These acts pitted Jesus against the religious authorities and ultimately against the foreign occupation forces who conspired to kill him.[10] The Chinese Christians found that the same kind of solidarity with their people led them to oppose foreign domination and to cooperate in the new common program for national independence and land reform.

War in Korea brought a sudden and total cut-off of foreign subsidies to the church, and self-support, self-government, and self-propagation became a reality even before the Three-Self Movement could be formally established to foster it.[11] During the next six to eight years the Three-Self Movement took the place of the old Council of Churches, working tirelessly to educate and consolidate the churches and seminaries to live within their greatly reduced means and yet make a positive contribution to China's reconstruction. Already by 1954 one can see in church documents a shift in the Three-Self program from purification of the church to unity with respect for differences among Christians, and from fighting America to peacemaking.[12] But the exhaustion of the country that came from extreme efforts in the late 1950s to industrialize, from crop failures in the early 1960s, and finally from the Cultural Revolution through 1977, was very harsh on the churches and all other cultural institutions. By the time religious freedom was reestablished in the 1980s two things had happened. Western denominational forms had disappeared when each believer's life had narrowed itself down to a small locality where to find any other Christian was a joy. And China had begun to respect the Christians who had been persecuted among its other religious and intellectual leaders. The China Christian Council was formed 1980 to coordinate church nurture toward full unity, working very slowly by local experiments so as not to alienate distinctive church groups.[13] This freed the Three-Self Movement to operate as liaison with the wider society, recovering church buildings, monitoring religious freedom, and working for peace and social welfare. The church is now at home in China and able to be a significant force, in some rural areas even a powerful force, for new life.

IS GOD OBSOLETE?

A miniature picture of China's rural church today is provided in a recent study by the Shanghai Social Science Institute of a specific town in Anhui province.[14] Only a few older women here were known as Christians during the Cultural Revolution, and they were pressed into attending political classes and doing many unwanted tasks. With the return of religious freedom these women received a wide hearing and in a few years the church included eight hundred people, about 25 percent between thirty and fifty years of age and 20 percent under thirty. There is one Bible, from which a literate local man or woman will read and interpret at length a short passage each Sunday to the outdoor gathering. This speaking alternates with informal individual and group singing, favoring local ballads about people practicing service and filial piety. During the long closing prayer by the leader, most pray their own prayers softly, and some with special needs plead more loudly. There is no clergy, offering, or holy meal. Some male believers are not present and gatherings may be moved to the evening if the crops require more people's time. Christians are preferred as neighbors because people think they are honest in business and decent in family life. Though the church has no healing services, about half the worshippers said they came to believe due to illness in the family and a number tell healing stories about long-time sicknesses now gone.

In closing this study the Chinese sociologists try to explain their findings. They think the increase in social well-being can account for the physical healings claimed. And they think the church's growth can be explained partly as a popular reaction to the excesses of the Cultural Revolution, partly from the lack of hospitals and sufficient education in small towns, and partly because of the Christians' mutual support and future hope. They assure us that, once education and economic development provide the strong base for a modern society, the primitive measures of the church will no longer interest people.

I find this account fascinating for many reasons — the faithful and dynamic women, the people's expositions of the Bible, the ballads, the miracle stories — all signs of the people's power in their own idiom. But I have time to consider only one aspect — the sociologists' dilemma reflected at the article's end. Are they right that this power of the people will become obsolete when hospitals and schools and educated leadership finally arrive in town? This is not only what Communist ideology teaches, but it is also the unspoken assumption of the capitalist priority on economic development. Any *theology* of power must face the question whether the people's demand to be sane, free of harassment, fed, and well has found an economic and political solution in our time that makes its religious expression redundant.

On the one hand we must concede that miracle telling has its social context in deprivation and that penicillin, self-rule, and good diet do well to supplant it. In other words, progress is possible in the people's demands to be well, in their taking up the divine challenge to feed themselves, determine right from wrong, and struggle against evil. The divine power put at human disposal is more than happy to be applied with foresight and evaluation. But no one who has lived with open eyes in our century can say that "the kingdoms of this world have become the kingdom of our God." Technology has brought longer life and mass death. This makes social organization crucial to control development, but neither of the two dominant forms of social organization in our world has learned how to facilitate consistently the people's power to meet their own basic needs.

To return to the specific town in Anhui Province and other scattered points of light in East and West, what is the prognosis? When doctors, educators, and clergy reach communities like these, will the people be increasingly empowered? The answer is by no means certain, since all such professional groups tend to operate like the Pharisees in Jesus' time to justify themselves by the inadequacy of others. Yet many people are working to cultivate a very different kind of indigenous leader today, as is the Chinese church. Meanwhile it seems to me quite appropriate to take this church of eight hundred people in Anhui Province *as it is* to be a sign for us of God's spirit now as always at work, provoking people to realize the power God gives in every place. May the gospel be so active in places like this that the doctors from the university and the teachers from the normal schools and the clergy from the seminaries may find their discouragement at being sent to such a place suddenly turn to recognition that God is present there, then to repentance and to solidarity with the people in the struggle to claim and use well the power that God is always eager to give us. And let us have no fear about God's obsolescence when the work of salvation is done. Are we falling back into the role of the authorities who worry that they must protect God from being used up by the needs of the people?

One final story. When the first American electronics factory was built in Kuala Langat in the Selangor district of Malaysia, the management hired young girls from nearby villages to do the precision work.[15] Their families were glad to have the added income, $3.00 to $4.00 U.S. a day. Hours were long, days off few, and they were expected to work faster once they had finished training. One day a girl went into a fit, screaming and loosing control of her body, and by the end of the week the same thing had happened to several others. Later in the month there was mass hysteria and the factory floor had to be closed down. Girls said they had seen spirits in the microscopes and the village elders announced that there was an evil spirit in the plant. The management was compelled to give a week medical leave and a local *imam* was sent to ritually clean the factory premises before the girls would return. The girls came back rested, but the process happened again when they became too tired. Tell me, is there an evil spirit in that plant? Will the union, if they ever get one, deal with it much more wisely than the girls and their *imam*? And if a union does serve the people better, will that be any less God's work?

Notes

1. Philostratus, *Life of Apollonius of Tyana* (Cambridge: Harvard University Press, and London: Heinemann, 1969), 4.10, 25; cf. 4.13.

2. *Babylonian Talmud, Baba Mezia* 59ab; cf. *Jerusalem Talmud, Mo'ed Katan* 3.1; G. Vermes in *Jesus the Jew* (London: Collins, 1973; Philadelphia: Fortress, 1981), 58–85, sets Jesus in the context of other miracle-working rabbis, especially Hanina ben Dosa. For the text of the Eliezer story and further delineation of the four types of gospel stories see my "The Gospel Miracle Stories and Their Tellers," *Semeia* 11 (1978): 83–113.

3. Theories proposing that these silencings are literary additions for a theological purpose do not explain equally well all their appearances in Mark. The strongest hypothesis seems to be that a silencing indigenous to some stories has been extended to others by Mark as part of his depiction of Jesus (see Wire, ibid., 104–5).

4. For further development of this typology see A. Wire, "The Gospel Miracle Story as the Whole Story," *South East Asia Journal of Theology* (now *East Asia Journal of Theology*) 22, no. 2 (October 1981): 29–37.

5. Huang Peixin, "Why Are You Crying?" (translations of

Chinese titles are mine), *Tian Feng* 409–10 (April 13, 1954): 207. Articles in Chinese-titled journals below are all in Chinese.

6. For this kind of interpretation of the gospels, see the editorial series on the gospel of Luke, which began in 1949 and continued through 1950, in *Tian Feng*, especially "A Voice in the Wilderness," 199 (February 4, 1950): 48–49; "The Gospel of Revolution," 200 (February 11, 1950): 60–61; "Reform the Church," 207 (April 1, 1950): 144; and "Woe to You Pharisees," 209 (April 15, 1950). See also Y. T. Wu's "The Truth Will Make You Free," *Tian Feng* 396–97 (January 11, 1954): 3–5; "Who Nailed Jesus to the Cross?" *Tian Feng* 400 (February 1, 1954): 56–60; and "All Good Comes from God," *Tian Feng* 402 (February 22, 1954): 90–93 (the first and third of these essays and a summary of the second are in English in *Documents of the Three-Self Movement: Source Materials for the Study of the Protestant Church in Communist China* (National Council of Churches in the USA, 1963), 78–84, edited — and sometimes translated — from an American viewpoint).

7. The background and significance of the manifesto are described by Y. T. Wu in "Unfurling the Banner of the Church Reform Movement," *Tian Feng* 233–34 (September 30, 1950): 155–60. For the manifesto itself see *Documents*, 19–20.

8. "Woe to You Pharisees," *Tian Feng* 209 (April 13, 1950). The issues of *Tian Feng* in 1951 and 1952 contain numerous self-criticisms; see *Documents*, 51–69.

9. "Let the Ear That Can Hear, Hear!" *Tian Feng* 204 (March 11, 1950): 109.

10. Ding Guanxun (Bishop K. H. Ting), "Why Still Want to Be a Preacher Today?" *Jinling Xiehe Shenxue Zhi* 2 (April 1954): 60–67; Sun Hanshu, "The Crowd Went Ahead and Before Praising the Lord," *Jinling Xiehe Shenxue Zhi* 4 (November 1955): 17–19; Gao Yucong, "Jesus Christ's Model for Loving One's Country," *Jinling Xiehe Shenxue Zhi* 7 (August 1957): 4–5. An English translation by Yao Niangeng of parts of the first article by Bishop K. H. Ting is available under the title "Why Be a Minister?" in *No Longer Strangers: Selected Writings by K. H. Ting*, edited by Raymond L. Whitehead (Maryknoll, N.Y.: Orbis Books, 1989), 85–89.

11. This is reflected in the church declaration after the Beijing Conference in April 1951, *Tian Feng* 262–63 (May 8, 1951):

198–99, *Documents*, 41–42, and in Y. T. Wu's subsequent "The Chinese Church's New Life," *Tian Feng* 266 (June 2, 1951): 261–64.

12. Y. T. Wu, "Four-Year Report on the Chinese Christian Three-Self Movement," *Tian Feng* 425–27 (September 3, 1954): 431–38; Y. T. Wu, "Report to Second National Conference," *Tian Feng* 502 (April 16, 1956): 7–14. These appear in English in *Documents*, 85–95, 121–33. For a careful analysis of the Three-Self Movement in its political context see Philip Lauri Wickeri, *Seeking the Common Ground: Protestant Christianity, the Three-Self Movement and China's United Front* (Maryknoll, N.Y.: Orbis Books, 1988).

13. The founding of the China Christian Council is described in Zheng Jianye, "On the Question of a Church Affairs Organization," *Chinese Theological Review 1985*, Foundation for Theological Education in South-East Asia, 1985, 42–48. Shen Derong explained the care the church has taken as it moves toward a stronger unity during an interview with a San Francisco Theological Seminary delegation at the Shanghai Three-Self Movement office in June 1987.

14. Zheng Kaitang, "The Soil That Makes Religion Grow," in *Zhongguo Shehuizhuyi Shiqi de Zongjiao Wenti* (The Religious Question in China's Socialist Period, in Chinese only), Luo Zhufeng, ed. (Shanghai Institute for Social Science, 1987), 257–67.

15. Aihwa Ong, "Global Industries and Malay Peasants in Peninsular Malaysia," *Women, Men, and the International Division of Labor* (Albany, N.Y.: State University of New York Press, 1983), 434–35 and 440–41; *Asiaweek*, August 4, 1978.

5

RECLAIMING A THEOLOGY OF GLORY FROM THE CORINTHIAN WOMEN PROPHETS

Antoinette Clark Wire

It is a truism today that people of different cultures have distinct experiences of God and, consequently, different theologies. The Cook Lectures, which from the 1920s to the 1960s were delivered in Asia each decade by a white male North American theologian, now in 1988 are offered in the United States and Asia by a Ghanaian scholar of African religions, a Korean *minjung* theologian, and an American feminist New Testament teacher. But do such voices from the periphery of traditional Western theology have anything substantively different to say? Is this "rainbow theology" simply a more colorful refraction of the familiar white beam, the better to attract various eyes to its light? Or does the rainbow articulate essentially different positions that must not be reabsorbed? If so, we will be working strategically, each in our own way, to redefine theological reflection in terms of the social position and struggle that characterizes our experience. Only such constructive work will retire the theology of universal ideas that justifies given structures and powers.

Different social positions have meant substantially different confessions of Christ from the very beginning of the church. I take as a demonstration of this the conflict that appears in 1 Corinthians between the theology of Paul and that of the Corinthian women prophets as I reconstruct them.[1] My thesis is that Paul, who has significant social privilege, finds himself experiencing a major loss of

social status in Christ. He takes this as the measure of following Christ who, though equal with God, did not assert
his status but emptied himself to become a human being
and ultimately to be crucified. But those in Corinth who
lack privilege in education, social power, family name, and
gender, have no such status to give up and do not respond
to Paul's "theology of the cross." With Christ's humiliation already built into their lives, they find their social
position rising in Christ and they call others into Christ's
resurrection glory.

RHETORICAL ANALYSIS

We meet both these confessions of Christ in the New Testament. But Paul's is the viewpoint of the writer, and it
has dominated Western readings of the Bible, especially
in Protestantism after Luther, who used Paul's theology to
undermine Roman hegemony in the church. The recent
ascendancy of literary analysis in biblical interpretation
has only intensified this absorption with the author's
viewpoint.

Meanwhile historians have discovered that, since writing in most societies has been a privilege of the few, we
see through their texts a view of social life from the top
down. In the Roman East only a small percentage of people could write,[2] so whatever is written bears this socially
specific view of the subject at hand. This is particularly
important to remember in the case of the New Testament
writers because, in contrast to some ancient authors, they
do speak about and address others who do not themselves
write. The challenge is to find a method to recover reliable
historical data from such a text, including data about the
point of view of the nonwriters involved. This does not
of course replace the task of getting an accurate reading
of the author's point of view, since it is our entré into the
situation.

My approach in studying the Corinthian women prophets has been that of rhetorical criticism. Paul is address-
ing the Corinthians in this letter in order to influence them,

to persuade them, and this puts certain constraints on him. For example, he cannot be persuasive if he appeals to facts about them that are patently false. So when he says, "Not many of you were wise . . . , not many powerful, not many of known families," he is probably reflecting the actual conditions of their lives at the time they were converted. What he says in this way about the Corinthian Christians in general, as well as in other statements about Corinthian women and about Corinthian prophets, can all be used to build a picture of the Corinthian women prophets in this church. It is of course possible that he is not well informed, but his own project of persuading them can be counted on to motivate him to the best possible use of his multiple sources of data about them.

A second, broader method of rhetorical analysis is to take everything Paul says as an effort to persuade his audience and therefore an indication of what they have not yet agreed to, what warrants they find persuasive in what combinations, and what tone and emphasis they are susceptible to. Although, if tightly construed, this approach assumes falsely that everything the writer says will persuade the intended readers, it nonetheless provides very precise and subtle indicators of a great deal that the writer understands about them. Except where there are reasons to the contrary, this information can be assumed to apply to groups known to be within his audience such as the Corinthian women prophets.

Even if it is possible to reconstruct the voices of non-writers of the New Testament such as the Corinthian women prophets, some will contest their authority as canonical voices or even declare them heretical wherever they deviate from the writer. But the New Testament itself speaks for a broader view of its own authority than that of a divine oracle for a writer. Its multiple authorship relativizes the viewpoint of any one author, its form of narrative and argument clearly seeks to induce belief rather than to pronounce dicta, and its content says that God alone is absolute authority and judge. Paul himself attests to the authority of the prophets in the early church, including Corinth, and nowhere claims that the written form of a statement is what makes it authoritative. Finally, historical research indicates that the earliest faith in Christ was that of nonwriters. In contexts where nonwriters disagree with writers, it is therefore important to reconstruct each viewpoint in relation to the social position of its proponents and to consider the authority of each voice.

WOMEN'S LOT

To provide some broader historical context for this study of the Corinthian women prophets, I select one element of Greek life recently under discussion by social historians. The standard method of birth control was infanticide, the exposure of infants. The cost to women of this kind of birth control was very high.[3] Because only the well-off could afford the dowry necessary for a daughter's wedding whereas sons could be expected to earn money, almost all the babies exposed were girls. Some did not die because they were found and raised to be prostitutes or slaves. The girl who was not exposed was married at an average age of twelve to a man about twenty. This early marriage and the quick remarriage of widows happened not only because of tradition but also because there were two few girls who survived birth for the number of men. Girls had no time to get an education beyond how to care for the open hearth. Once married, a girl had to give birth to at least three children for every two that would survive. This, in conjunction with minimal health care, led to many childbirth deaths and a life expectancy for women about seven years less than that of men. Perhaps worst of all, the father alone decided whether or not a child could live. This shows in one key aspect the life of the Corinthian women — under immediate threat of death at birth and again at childbirth, with prostitution or slavery for those who survived exposure and early marriage without decision-making power in the family for the others.

We know that there were women prophets in Corinth because Paul says to them that women who pray and prophesy with heads uncovered shame their heads (11:5).

On the basis of Paul's statement, most readers picture the women in Corinth dutifully covered and, according to 1 Corinthians 14:35, silent in the assembly. Then, to justify Paul's restrictions, some immoral or pagan practice among them is assumed, though Paul makes no such accusation. In fact, Paul's argument that they should cover their heads is our best evidence that they did not. His question, "Judge for yourselves, is it proper for a woman to pray uncovered?" shows he assumes they know that bare heads are not standard practice. And his closing sentence in this argument, "If anyone wants to make an issue of this, we recognize no other practice," shows he is expecting them to oppose covering their heads. These women's bare heads are not an accident due to differences in dress code between Jews and Gentiles but a statement that has some particular meaning for the prophesying women. Paul argues here from parity — men are obligated not to cover their heads; women are obligated to cover their heads — suggesting that the women he wants to persuade are interested in being treated fairly vis-à-vis the men. It could be precisely this interest that makes the women adopt the male practice of not covering their heads.

PAUL'S ARGUMENT

The reason for this claim to parity is indicated when Paul brings in the Genesis creation story. To convince them to cover their heads he first says that man is the head of the woman, probably an allusion to Eve's being told after the fall, "He shall rule over you" (Gen. 3:16). Yet this argument from the consequence of sin seems insufficiently strong and he goes on to argue that man is God's image. Although Genesis speaks inclusively of creation "in God's image...male and female" (Gen. 1:27), Paul contrasts the man as "God's image and glory" with the woman as "man's glory" (1 Cor. 11:7), using a rabbinical tradition that allowed a man to divorce a wife who was "not his glory."[4] Paul's position seems to be that everyone can worship better, including even the angelic host, if

the male prophesies uncovered, since he directly reflects
God's image and glory. But the woman, whom Paul claims
reflects man's glory, is better covered so as not to distract
the angels, or — perhaps more to the point — the men,
whose distraction may be what Paul really understands.[5]

Whether this dress is better for the women's worship
he does not consider. Paul's peculiar argument that the
woman, made from man's rib and for his sake (Gen.
2:22), "ought to have authority on her head for the angels' sake" makes sense only if he is quoting something
they have already heard. He clearly means "authority" as
head-covering, a sign of the man's authority over her. But
the phrase about her "having authority on her head for
the angels' sake" is in its own right a positive authority
claim and suggests that the women were claiming authority to bare their heads when worshipping God among
the angels. They may have shared a common Jewish and
Christian view that the angels are praising God eternally,
day and night. Their claim to have authority in Christ to
join this circle of praise may also be in Paul's mind later
when he criticizes those who "speak in the tongues of humans and of angels" (1 Cor. 13:1), as well as when he tries
to persuade the Corinthians throughout this letter not to
make use of their authority in Christ (6:12–13; 9:12, 18;
10:23–28).

But what does this authority to worship God among
the angels mean to them? The fact that Paul chooses
to use Genesis — which speaks of a creation in God's
image of male and female — to argue to the contrary for
head-covering as a sign of woman's subordination to man
suggests that in this passage as a whole he is reinterpreting
their positive claims. They could be quoting the full sentence from Genesis that Paul is rebutting, "And God made
the human being; according to the image of God he made
him; male and female he made them" (Gen. 1:27; similarly
5:1b–2). Or they could be using some early Christian re-
formulation of this statement. What immediately comes to
mind is the Christian confession that was apparently used,
at least in the churches founded by Paul, whenever people were baptized. It appears three times in Pauline letters

and itself quotes from the Genesis text where italicized: "We who are baptized put on Christ, the new human being made *according to the image of God,* where there is neither Greek nor Jew, neither slave nor free, not *male and female,* but all one in Christ" (variously transmitted in Gal. 3:27–28, 1 Cor. 12:12–13, and Col. 3:9–11).[6]

If Paul is dealing with Genesis in order to contest this baptismal confession as it was understood by some Corinthian women, it becomes very important to reconstruct the meaning it had in Corinth. They claimed to have put on a new identity in Christ. This confession apparently functioned as their new creation story, redefining who they were and what they were created to do. The parts of the statement that were quoted from the old creation story, "made according to the image of God" and "male and female," are the traditional elements being reinterpreted in this new creation context. In contrast to the old creation, the image of God is now identified as Christ, a corporate reality in whom all are made one, not by a divine apotheosis but as the new human being, as true humanity realized in their common life.

The second phrase generating the Christian baptismal confession "male and female" shows that the new creation story was fully inclusive, or perhaps we should say exclusive, since it is now prefixed by a negative particle. Christ, God's image, is *not* male and female. But this cannot have meant that no men and no women could enter this life in Christ. Some argue that the new identity not male and female meant the restoration of an androgynous humanity that is both male and female, which in some Jewish texts and later Christian Gnostic texts is understood to antedate the fall of the divine spirit of humanity into physical, sexually differentiated bodies.[7]

But probably already before Paul's use, phrases like "neither Jew nor Greek, neither slave nor free" had been added, showing that the early and constant Christian meaning of "not male and female" during this period was social.[8] Those in Christ did not share in the major social divisions that cut across all humanity to privilege some groups at the expense of others — male over female, free over slave, Jew over Greek. The fact that the creation in God's image, male and female, was corrected into "*not male and female*" suggests that it had come to be used to legitimate women's social and religious subordination, as Paul in his argument for head-covering demonstrates.

And what had happened to Paul here? He was the one who had affirmed the new baptismal identity in Galatia in order to defend the Gentiles against subordination to the Jews (Gal. 3:23–29). But when he quotes the baptismal affirmation in Corinth he changes its meaning and uses it to defend the interdependence of different kinds of people in one body, not the cancelling of distinct identities, and he omits all reference to male and female: "For in one spirit we were all baptized into one body, whether Jews or Greeks, whether slaves or free, and we all drink from one spirit" (1 Cor. 12:13). Apparently Paul did not want to make any allusion to the cancelling of male privilege in a context where greater subordination of women was important to him. This study cannot focus on his reasons for this. But his arguments from immorality and idolatry suggest that he may have been trying to stop some offense that Jewish-Christians had taken to his Gentile gospel as practiced in Corinth (chapters 5, 6, 8, 10).

At one point in the argument on head-covering Paul seems to reverse himself: "But in the Lord a woman is not independent of man nor man of woman. For just as the woman is made from the man, so man is made through the woman, and all things are from God" (11:11–12). Such interdependence of the sexes in the Lord, based on woman's priority in the birth process that balances man's priority in the creation process, gives the appearance of parity to strengthen Paul's argument for head-covering among those who seek parity. But it defines woman's positive contribution in terms of the birth of sons.

MARRIAGE IN CORINTH

The problematic of this for women prophets in Corinth is that many of them have withdrawn from sexual relations with men to devote themselves to the gospel. This is apparent in Paul's seventh chapter, where he mentions women who have denied sex within marriage, others who have divorced believers or nonbelievers, and still others who have remained virgins or widows by choice. Although Paul himself had first set the example for the single life in Corinth and in this letter still advocates it as an ideal, because of sexual offenses in the Corinthian church he is advising that people who had chosen continence be remarried or married (5:1–7:2). Since all the people he charges with sexual offenses are males committing incest or adultery, taking each other to court for "defrauding," and going to prostitutes, the continent people Paul is persuading to marry them to end this immorality must be female. That he is working primarily to persuade women to be open to such marriage is also reflected in chapter 7 in his heaviest arguments from parity in the letter.[9]

For the women who prophesy, such marrying is not just a problem of conflicting personal commitments. All the women prophets mentioned in the New Testament are described by the writers in terms of their sexual practice. Hannah and the daughters of Philip are recognized as chaste and respected as prophets and Jezebel is called immoral and a false prophet (Luke 2:36–38; Acts 21:9; Rev. 2:20–25). The sexual life of New Testament male prophets is not discussed except as Paul uses himself as an example. Greek practice required continence for some women prophets such as the Pythia at Delphi and temporary periods of abstinence for many women officiating at festivals, practices less common for Greek men.[10] It is probable that a woman in Corinth would no longer be credible as a prophet once married, being considered, as Paul puts it, anxious about how "to please her husband" rather than how "to be holy in body and spirit," a phrase he does not apply to the men (7:32–34). Apparently in a society where women were subordinate in so many ways to men, prophecy was considered unreliable if a woman could have been influenced by a man rather than by God, if she had become part of the world of power manipulation rather than being open to the divine spirit. Paul's resort to marriage to solve the problem of male sexual offenses in the Corinthian church would have been a clear threat to women's leadership. At the same time his effort shows us that women in Corinth at the time he was writing were building an unusual life independent of men, perhaps some of them living with the widows, a practice later mentioned by the writer of 1 Timothy (1 Tim. 5:3, 9–14).

The radical nature of this change in their sexual lives, however, does not necessarily prove, as some have argued, that they understood "not male and female" in terms of return to an original androgyny before physical sexuality.[11] Because this myth is not explicitly attested in 1 Corinthians or in the first-century church, it is more appropriate to assume that their singleness functioned for them somewhat as Paul's did for him — as a total commitment, with the added very important difference that they chose this life when in a state of sexual dependence. To them it therefore carried an added meaning of assuring the freedom from subordination necessary for mediating God's word.[12]

PROPHECY AND TONGUES

The women's spiritual leadership becomes visible in Paul's arguments about gifts and prophecy. At great length he argues that gifts are distributed individually and make people dependent on each other, either mutually so, as organs in a human body, or by a certain subordination according to Paul's conclusion, "God set up in the church first apostles, second prophets, third teachers..." (12:28). His persistence in this point suggests that they do not already experience the Spirit distributing gifts among individuals. They may well see all believers receiving the potential for every spiritual manifestation. If so, they find their oneness in Christ by stimulation of every good gift in each person rather than by dependence, mutual or hierarchical. This would mean that the benefits of the Spirit come to them not primarily as recipients of what the Spirit does through others but as they themselves act as instruments of the Spirit in a context of common expectation.

Most fruitful for understanding the women's prophecies is Paul's development of the hierarchy of gifts into an extended contrast between prophecy and speaking in tongues (14:1–40). He argues that only prophecy is constructive in the community because it evokes God's presence so that people come to believe (14:24–25), whereas speaking in tongues is confusing, irrational, and immature. He applies to tongues the verbs "thank," "pray," "bless," and "sing" (14:14–17), showing that this speech was normally the language of prayer. And he proposes that, where no interpreter is present, it be addressed to God privately. Prophecy and prayer were apparently the primary elements in Corinthian worship — it was these two acts that Paul did not want the women to do uncovered — and Paul seeks the leverage to retire one by glorifying the other.

Paul's effort to separate ecstatic prayer and prophecy would only make sense if they were integral to each other in Corinth. Apparently the Corinthian prophets alternated freely between speaking God's words to the people — which was prophecy — and speaking the people's often ecstatic responses to God — which was prayer. We know they sometimes spoke communally and at length, with voices overlapping and without stopping for explanations, because Paul instructs them to speak one by one, no more than three in one session, always interpreting tongues and evaluating prophecies. He reassures them more than once that his "constructive" worship still allows for each to speak, for all to prophesy (14:24, 26, 31) — one assumes he means their turn will come. Apparently Paul expects opposition to his restricting the number of speakers. Their practice of worship must be communal, very broadly participatory, not at all "two or at most three" speaking in tongues, "one" interpreting and then "two or three" prophesying. It appears that the prophets in Corinth were not three or even a dozen people but a mass, credibly summarized by the word "all." As a whole, Paul's argument shows that he puts the priority on their attentive listening to a few and reflecting through a few, whereas they see themselves not primarily as hearers but as active mediators in the event of worship.

For our understanding of these women prophets it is crucial that just after Paul silences all noninterpreted speaking in tongues and all extended or overlapping prophecy he says, "Let the women be silent in the churches, for it is not proper for them to speak but to be subordinate as the law also says" (14:34). Paul then strengthens his credibility by a concession that gives nothing away, "But if any want to learn, let them ask their own men at home, for it is shameful for a woman to speak in church" (14:35).

Some have said Paul could not have written these two lines because he said earlier that women should cover their heads when they prophesy, which means they must have been speaking. Of course they were speaking or he would not be silencing them. The question is whether Paul could at one time insist they cover their heads when speaking and then forbid their speaking altogether. In fact individual arguments in Paul's letters often cannot be made consistent with each other, though they do finally point in the same direction. Eating food offered to idols is to be avoided because it endangers the eaters who devote to demons — even to nonexistent ones — what should be devoted to God (10:14–22). A few lines later such eating endangers only the observer who might believe in demons and is no problem for the persons themselves (10:23–30). But both arguments on idol food point in the same direction of caution about such eating. And both arguments about women point in the direction of restricting their participation in congregational speech.

Others argue that Paul didn't write these two verses silencing women because they appear at the chapter's end in some "Western" manuscripts and not at the location we find them. This could mean they were an addition in the margin after Paul's writing, then inserted differently into the text by two copyists. But the same manuscript tradition that puts these verses at the end of the chapter also makes a number of other obvious corrections of this part of the 1 Corinthians text, for example a few verses later reading "eleven" rather than "twelve" apostles who saw the resurrected Lord. All manuscripts before the twelfth century other than this Latin-related "Western group" include 14:34–35 in its numerical order, and efforts to relieve Paul of responsibility for these lines have no solid textual basis.

Finally others argue Paul could not have said these words because they do not belong in a chapter about prophecy and tongues, or, more broadly, do not belong in this letter or in Paul's overall conduct toward women. All of these arguments suffer from a faulty reading of 1 Corinthians, which evades or belittles the significance of women's role in Paul's writing.

PAUL'S DEMANDS

If Paul then did demand silence from the women at the climax of his argument to distinguish prophecy from tongues, it is almost certain that the women who prophesied were not only vocal but were particularly prone to incorporate ecstatic praise into their prophecies. His appeal to propriety — it is "not proper" but "shameful" for women to speak in the gatherings — shows that they had respect in the churches and among themselves, and he could therefore appeal to them on such grounds. Paul's concession that they ask at home if they want to learn has sometimes been taken to imply that they were primarily interested in asking questions. But a concession operates by making what is offered seem like what is wanted. In fact Paul has just said that "learning" will happen when they begin to prophesy one by one (14:31), so it is probably more his agenda than theirs, or at least they associate learning with all of them prophesying rather than with listening to others or asking them questions.

Paul's words after his silencing of women, as with his curt cut-off in the argument on head covering (11:16), are sharp and final. "Did God's word originate from you? or did it reach you people only?" (14:36) are rhetorical questions contrasting their local work with his broad mission enterprise and belittling their own claim to be a source and goal of God's word. Finally he challenges the prophets and spirituals to recognize his words as the Lord's command or no longer be recognized as prophets (14:37–38). This would perhaps be tolerable for the male prophets, who would then have to shape their prophecy in a more discursive way. But the women are being pressed to accept the silencing of their prophetic voices as a condition of their prophetic recognition — which is no recognition at all.

Although this challenge to the prophets to accept Paul's restrictions is rhetorical, followed as it is by "Whoever does not recognize this is not recognized" (14:37–38), nonetheless it reveals that the ultimate authority, even in rhetoric, is not Paul's own but the Spirit's as it speaks in himself and the prophets. Unfortunately there is no direct witness whether the prophets and spirituals in Corinth confirmed these restrictions or rejected them. Because women are no longer singled out for restriction in 2 Corinthians, are we to assume they are silent? Or does the strong evidence in 2 Corinthians of an escalating conflict between Paul and Corinth show that Paul's restrictions on them were rejected by the Spirit in the Corinthian prophets? If so, he changes his strategy in 2 Corinthians and chooses other apparently more effective means of persuasion than isolating the women.

Immediately after silencing the women and calling for good order in the church Paul turns to defending the future resurrection of the dead against some in Corinth who deny it. Can this group include the Corinthian women prophets? He begins by reciting the common confession of Christ's death, burial, and resurrection in sequence, which accentuates the resurrection appearances as historical events. Remarkably, in contrast to other early witnesses, he omits the first appearance to the women and/or their witness of the empty tomb, and he includes himself as one who received the last, unexpected appearance some years later. The Corinthians, who also believe in a risen Jesus (as Paul's continuing argument from that premise shows), may reject both his effort at historical credibility that leads to lists and to omitting women as primary witnesses, and his presentation of himself as the final witness as if they had no experience of the risen Christ. This would be consistent with their denying the resurrection of the dead in favor of the rising of the living, rejecting delay to the realm of the dead of what is already being realized in their life in Christ.

Paul pictures Christ's resurrection here as a past event that makes the church dependent on the apostles' witness (including his own) and that will not be realized in them until after death is overcome. He reinterprets the future resurrection of the dead in terms of the language of the baptismal experience — "being raised a spiritual body," "bearing the image of the heavenly one" who is also called "the second human being from heaven," "putting on immortality." This robs the believer of all the present claims of the baptismal confession, including, it seems, the identity that is "not male and female" that comes when one puts on the new human being raised from death. Paul tries to persuade them with a prophetic oracle: "Behold, I tell you a mystery, we will not all die but we will all be changed, in a second, in the wink of an eye, at the last trumpet...." Whether due to Paul's shock at widespread deaths of believers, to intimations of his own death, or to his judgment that the Corinthians are not yet living beyond death, Paul projects his conviction of the human rising in Christ into the future as resurrection of the dead, leaving the present as a time for all people in Christ to learn the way to death on the cross.

DIFFERENT SOCIAL EXPERIENCE

The Corinthian women prophets do not share his experience or his theology. At baptism they both died and were raised with Christ, and Christ's resurrection being realized among them stimulates gifts previously unknown, so that the once dispossessed now are generating a new kind of common life not found elsewhere (4:17; 7:17; 11:16; 14:33b). It is time for modern interpreters to stop imitating and even surpassing Paul's rhetoric in our condescending talk about the "presumptuous self-affirmations" of the "Corinthian elite." In this way we instinctively join Paul as the old elite in attacking the rising hordes of his time. To get a reasonably sympathetic reading of their thought and action we must better understand the role of social position in theology.

One step in this direction is to be more precise in identifying some aspects of the social experience of Paul and the Corinthian women prophets that are reflected in their respective understandings of Christ. I use "social experience" here to refer to a change of social status across multiple indicators. Both in order not to import into their setting inappropriate modern categories and in order to use the data in fact available, I take six different social indicators mentioned by Paul to gauge social status, once before they enter this community, then at the time of writing. When Paul says "neither Jew nor Greek, neither slave nor free, not male and female" (Gal. 3:28), he refers to the three factors of ethnic group security and status, condition of servitude or caste, and gender status. And when he says, "Look at your calling, brethren, that not many were wise by human standards, not many powerful, not many of known families" (1 Cor. 1:26), he speaks of the three factors of education, social influence, and family status.

Paul himself must be rated high on all six indicators before he entered the Christian community. He was from the Jewish ethnic group, which in Hellenistic cities of Asia had some independence and organization to take care of its own. He was free. He was male. His education within Judaism was formidable, whether you take Acts or strictly his letters as a gauge. His social influence in Judaism was significant enough for him to lead in certain persecutions of the church. And his family was well enough established in a Greek city to get him this education and influence; if Acts is followed he had probably inherited Roman citizenship. When he began to identify himself as a believer in Christ, his status fell overnight. Although he could not divest himself of inborn Jewishness, freedom, and male status, the normal privileges of being a free male Jew were compromised by his associations with Gentiles, slaves, and women in the new community. Jews with status considered that his education had been for nothing, he lost his social influence with them, and his family may have disowned him. His status did drop only partially in each indicator, since he was building some new influence in the small group and kept his citizenship, maleness, and freedom intact. But the social experience of voluntary loss was strong enough to focus his Christian faith on Christ Jesus' giving up divine privilege to become a human being and suffer crucifixion for others. To sin was to boast in one's own Jewish law or Greek wisdom, deny God's common judgment of all special privilege, and empty Christ's cross of its power to overcome privilege and reconcile all people to God. Focusing his eyes only on the Jew-Gentile division, he apparently saw the Corinthian women prophets as boasters in wisdom who would not give up exercising their authority in the risen Christ to stop offending Jews like himself.

But the prophesying Corinthian women had a very different social experience. At conversion they ranked very low in at least two of the first three social indicators. They were Greek rather than Jew in a once proud Greek city that two centuries before had been razed to the ground by the Romans and one century earlier rebuilt as a Roman colony and provincial capital. So as Greeks they lacked political organization, cultural pride, and religious ritual. As women they were of the "inferior sex," as the philosophers demurely put that threat to their lives. And in condition of servitude, demographers have estimated that Hellenistic cities were about one-third slave, more in a Roman colony, suggesting roughly one-half slave for a socially marginal group in that setting.[13] Hence they ranked very low in ethnic security, very low in gender, and about half of them very low in caste. And if Paul could say of all the Corinthian believers that when called to believe, "not many of you were wise . . . , not many powerful, not many of known families," certainly the women were those of lowest education and social power among them all. And only a very few can have come from families of status. In all, they lived short and harsh lives, taught from first breath to think themselves of no account, and a crucified Jesus would be no stranger among them.

But in Christ their lives opened into a new reality. Although a Christian woman on the street remained a Greek female slave, she had put on Christ, God's image, where there was no ethnic, caste, or gender discrimination. And the community that provoked her to practice her new identity did not meet weekly in some public building but daily in her own or her neighbor's home. The doors were open and strangers came in to wonder. Here were people without education and yet full of wisdom in Christ, without power and yet mediating between God and the people so that strangers were convicted to believe, without family connections and yet unmistakably God's own family "already ruling" in the kingdom (4:10). People once immobilized in humiliation and self-abnegation — not like Paul in pride and boasting — experienced salvation in Christ not as Paul did in relinquishing special privilege and learning the way of the cross but in gaining a new identity. Greek slave women risen in Christ were drawing the whole world into God's image. This was their experience of the risen Christ and their participation in God's glory. They would not lightly set down this life because someone else's experience of Christ had been different.

CONFLICT AS WITNESS

There are two ways we can resolve the tension of this conflict in our history. On the one hand we can stay as close as possible to Paul's view, conceding perhaps that the women prophets' social position gave them more justification for their rising in Christ than Paul allowed, but yet concluding that their glory had gone too far and now needed his correction. Or we can side with the women on the assumption that the balance of power had not yet been sufficiently redressed and that his correction of them was premature. In either case this kind of analysis is based on what is sometimes called a structural-functionalist view of society, one that assumes that society is always changing in order to recover a functional balance between freedom and order, thought and emotion, and between any other forces that threaten to make it not work. The same perception could be stated philosophically by affirming a universal concept of human nature as both requiring leadership and participatory, so that extreme domination or subordination must be redressed to find an appropriate fulfillment of human nature.

Such theories as this are not without a measure of truth in that they conceive an ideal world that might inspire human effort or be reconceived as experience teaches. But their fatal weakness is to delude us into thinking, first, that the ideal is built in to society or nature and will achieve itself if all work for their enlightened self-interest. Second, it operates as if good is somehow half way between two evils and requires only an adjustment to be realized. Essentially this dignifies evil as only a step away from good, legitimates existing structures and powers as "on the way," and keeps people from taking the risks needed to reverse evil and realize good.

Therefore it is important *not* to resolve the conflict in our history that this study has revealed. On the contrary, it must stand as a witness. It is a witness in the first place to the work of Christ in human beings who have put on God's image where there is no Jew or Greek, slave or free, male or female. Having done this, Paul is beginning to learn the way of the cross, not only in the partial loss of social status, which he accepts as the price of his call to proclaim Christ crucified to the Gentiles, but also in threats to his new status as the apostle who will unite Jew and Gentile as God's people. Things are not going well in this calling. Certain Gentile believers in Corinth have other priorities and the Jews are opting out, leaving him with nothing visible for all his losses. He is tempted to settle in Corinth for the freedom of Jew and Gentile men in Christ. The way of the cross is deeper than he had thought.

The Corinthian women prophets are also a witness to the new life in Christ. They know Christ's death in the continuing social vulnerability of their lives so visible in this letter and are beginning to learn the way of his rising.

They witness to the freedom in Christ to leave sexual partners and live in a community without exploitation where they can join others in mediating God's word to the people and the people's pleas and praises to God. But their rising in Christ is under attack. Paul wants them to marry to make sexual life simpler for men, to cover their heads to make worship less distracting for men, and to be silent to keep the people's communication with God under the control of men. They apparently are not tempted to consent to this denial of the spirit of God in them and the conflict continues — against mounting forces.

The struggle reflected in 1 Corinthians is not only witness to the beginnings of God's own image in Christ being realized among human beings. It is also, and most poignantly, witness to the denial of this Christ image. Paul did try to cut his losses by a total silencing of the Corinthian women prophets, betraying his calling to include all Gentiles in God's image in Christ. As often with compromises, it did not ingratiate the Jews, if that was his purpose, and probably did not silence the women. But it pointed in a direction that others followed. This denial of God's image in these people positioned on the social margin quickly gained strength as the privileged found ways to stylize the way of the cross in terms of bishops' martyrdoms and cruciform churches. With some dependence on this letter, the way of the cross was consistently interpreted to mean social denial in the case of those who sought to rise from social exploitation. Their resurrection was delayed until Christ conquered death, as if that had not yet taken place. By this deceit, the power of death took on a new lease in the world.

Yet in spite of this, rumors and prophecies of the experience of a new humanity in Christ that is "neither Jew nor Greek, neither slave nor free, not male and female" have never completely died out, and this letter is one of the witnesses.

Notes

1. For a complete reconstruction see my *Corinthian Women Prophets: A Reconstruction through Paul's Rhetoric* (Minneapolis: Fortress Press, 1990).

2. This has recently been demonstrated by William V. Harris in *Ancient Literacy* (Cambridge, Mass., and London: Harvard University Press, 1989).

3. Sarah B. Pomeroy, "Infanticide in Hellenistic Greece," in A. Cameron and A. Kuhrt, eds., *Images of Women in Antiquity* (Detroit: Wayne State University Press, 1983), 207–22. For evaluations of the depopulation problem see Pomeroy, *Goddesses, Whores, Wives and Slaves: Women in Classical Antiquity* (New York: Schocken Books, 1975), 140; D. Engels, "The problem of Female Infanticide in the Greco-Roman World," *Classical Philology* 75, no. 2 (1980): 112–20; and W. V. Harris, "Infanticide in the Greco-Roman World," *Classical Quarterly* 32 (1982): 114–16. On marriage age see Pomeroy, *Goddesses*, 64; and Gerhard Delling, *Paulus' Stellung zu Frau und Ehe* (Stuttgart: Kohlhammer, 1931), 37 n. 349. Concerning the relative life expectancies of men and women, see Pomeroy, *Goddesses*, 179; and J. Laurence Angel, "Ecology and Population in the Eastern Mediterranean," *World Archeology* 4 (1972), 88–105, table 28.

4. *Talmud j Kethuboth* 3:34b; or in Jacob Neusner's translation, *The Talmud of the Land of Israel, Ketubot* 11:3 2CD: "The wife of R. Yose the Galilean gave him much grief. R. Eleazar b. Azariah went up to see him. He said to him, 'Rabbi, divorce her for she does not respect you [Aramaic: she is not your glory].' He said to him, 'Her marriage settlement is too much for me to pay.' He said to him, 'I'll give you what you need to pay off her marriage settlement, so you can divorce her.' He gave him what he needed to settle the marriage contract and he divorced her." Concerning the broader rabbinical context of Paul's argument here, Jervell points out that when Paul appeals to the male as God's image, he departs from the inclusive interpretation of Adam by some rabbis and from the Hellenistic Christian tradition shared by the Corinthians that identifies Christ and all in Christ as God's image. Paul, apparently in this context alone, picks up the branch of rabbinical exegesis that identifies only Adam and not Eve as God's image. See Jacob Jervell, *Imago Dei. Gen. 1, 26f im Spaetjudentum, in der*

Gnosis und in den paulinischen Briefen (Göttingen: Vandenhoeck and Ruprecht, 1960), 107–12, 296–303.

5. This general view is developed by M. D. Hooker in her "Authority on Her Head: An Examination of I Cor XI 10," *New Testament Studies* 10 (1963–64): 410–16.

6. These passages are widely recognized to reflect a Christian baptismal statement of pre-Pauline origin that Paul adapts for his uses. For analyses and literature see Hans Dieter Betz, *Galatians: A Commentary on Paul's Letter to the Churches in Galatia* (Philadelphia: Fortress, 1979), 181–201; Elisabeth Schüssler Fiorenza, *In Memory of Her: A Feminist Theological Reconstruction of Christian Origins* (New York: Crossroad, 1983), 205–36, 237 n. 12; Dennis Ronald MacDonald, *There Is No Male and Female: The Fate of a Dominical Saying in Paul and Gnosticism* (Philadelphia: Fortress, 1987), 5–14. The variety within the parallel three versions of the saying indicates that it was an oral rather than a written tradition, giving authors freedom to adapt further.

7. Wayne Meeks, "The Image of the Androgyne: Some Uses of a Religious Symbol in Earliest Christianity," *History of Religions* 13 (1974): 165–208; MacDonald, *There Is No Male and Female*, 65–126. This research builds on the foundation laid by Jacob Jervell in *Imago Dei*, 107–9, 161–65, 292–312, 332–36.

8. The other pairs beyond the original "male and female" taken from Genesis are very unlikely to be Paul's own additions because "neither slave nor free" in Galatians is not motivated by any apparent problem with the slaves or free in Galatia. Also it survives in 1 Corinthians, both in 12:12 and 7:12–24 (and even in Col. 3:11), as a more formally parallel than socially crucial part of the argument (against MacDonald, *There Is No Male and Female*, 121–23).

9. 1 Cor. 7:2, 3, 4, 10–11, 12–13, 14, 16, 26 (see Greek text in light of 7:1 and 25), 28, 32–34.

10. Plutarch, *The Oracles at Delphi*, 405CD; idem, *Obsolescence of Oracles*, 435D, 437D–438C; H. Strathmann, *Geschichte der fruehchristlichen Askese bis zur Entstehung des Moenchtums im religionsgeschichtlichen Zusammenhange, I. Die Askese in der Umgebung des werdenden Christentums* (Leipzig: A. Deichter'sche Verlagsbuchhandlung Werner School, 1914), 199–208.

11. See n. 5, above.

12. See Virginia Burrus, *Chastity as Autonomy* (Lewiston, N.Y.: Edwin Mellen Press, 1987); also Antoinette Wire, "'Women Consecrated in Body and Spirit': The Functions of Virginity among the Wise," in Karen King, ed., *Images of the Feminine in Gnosticism* (Philadelphia: Fortress, 1988).

13. Estimates of the slave population in the Roman East vary, some demographers talking of three slaves to a slave-holding family, not far from Galen's reference to one slave for every two free in second-century Pergamum (see Thomas Wiedemann, *Greek and Roman Slavery* [Baltimore: Johns Hopkins University Press, 1981], 5–6; W. C. Westermann, "Sklaverei," in *Real-Encyclopadie fuer Altertumswissenschaft* [Stuttgart, 1935], suppl. vol. 6: 894–95, 931–34, 999, 1002; M. I. Finley, *Ancient Slavery and Modern Ideology* [New York: Viking Press, 1980], 80). J. Beloch counts Rome as slightly over half-slave in 5 C.E. (*Die Bevoelkerung der griechisch-roemischen Welt* [Leipzig, 1886], 95ff. [cited in a good overview on slave-free ratios by Ulf-Ranier Kuegler, "Die Paränese an die Sklaven als Modell urchristlicher Sozialethik," dissertation, Friedrich-Alexander Universität, Erlangen-Nuernberg, 1977, 40–41, 290]).

CONTRIBUTORS

KOFI ASARE OPOKU was born in Ghana. He received his primary, secondary, and higher education in that country and was graduated with honors from the University of Ghana, Legon. He has done graduate theological studies at Yale University Divinity School and at the University of Bonn.

Professor Opoku teaches at the Institute of African Studies of the University of Ghana in the field of sociology of religion in Africa and in African traditional religions. His research interests are also in African ethics, religion and art in Africa, oral literature and history, and Akom culture.

His publications include *Traditional Religion* (Legon: Institute of African Studies, 1968), *Akom Ho Nkommobo* (Legon: Institute of African Studies, 1969), *Speak to the Winds: Proverbs from Africa* (New York: Lathrop, Lee and Shepard, 1975), and *West African Traditional Religion* (Singapore: Far Eastern Publishers, 1981). He has contributed chapters to nine books and published nearly three dozen articles on religion. He has been editor of the *Research Review* of the Institute of African Studies and is co-editor of *Odawuni*, an Akom scholarly magazine published by the Institute.

Professor Opoku has presented papers at numerous scholarly conferences in Africa, Europe, and North America on African traditional religion and culture, on black civilization, religion, philosophy, history, and education and their relation to Christian faith. He has lectured at more than fifteen colleges and universities in the United States and has often appeared on television and been heard on radio programs.

Professor Opoku is an active lay leader of the Presbyterian Church of Ghana and is vice moderator of the Sub-Unit of Dialogue of the World Council of Churches.

KIM YONG-BOCK was born in Korea and was graduated from Yonsei University, Seoul, in 1961. He has done graduate study at Princeton Theological Seminary, from which he received the degree of doctor of philosophy in 1976.

Dr. Kim serves at the Center for the Study of World Mission for Third World Church Leaders, where he lectures on *minjung* theology, social ethics, Third World theologies, ecumenical issues, and Korean Christianity. He concurrently is an adjunct faculty member for San Francisco Theological Seminary. He has also served as teaching fellow or visiting scholar at Princeton Theological Seminary, Tokyo Union Theological Seminary, and Sophia University, Seoul.

Dr. Kim has been actively associated with several ecumenical study and research centers. He served as Graduate School Tutor at the Ecumenical Institute in Bossey, Switzerland, in 1977–78, was founder and director of the Christian Institute for Study and Research, Seoul (1978–79), and co-director for research of the Christian Institute for the Study of Justice and Development, Seoul (1979–84). He has served as pastor of the Sandol Presbyterian Church, Seoul, since 1985.

Dr. Kim has had extensive ecumenical experience, having participated in the general assemblies of the Christian Conference of Asia, of the World Student Christian Federation, and of the World Council of Churches. He has served on the Theological Commission of CCA and on the World Council of Churches Unit on Justice and Service and its Commission on the Church's Participation in Development, of which he has been vice moderator since 1984. He has served on the staff of the Commission on Ecumenical Mission and Relations of the Presbyterian Church (U.S.A.) (1970–72), is a member of its Task Force on Catholicity, and is one of its Bi-National Servants.

Dr. Kim's writings include *Historical Transformation: People's Movement and Christian Koinonia* (1976). He was author and editor of CCA publications *Toiling under Phar-*

aoh (1977) and *Minjung Theology* (1980), and he has written *Korean Minjung and Theology* (1980), *Messiah and Minjung* (1986), and *Korean Minjung and Social Biography* (1987). He has contributed four dozen articles in Korean and English theological and ecumenical journals.

ANTOINETTE CLARK WIRE did her undergraduate studies at Pomona College in Claremont, California, and graduate theological study at the University of Bonn and Yale University Divinity School. She received her doctorate from the Claremont Graduate School in 1974.

Dr. Wire has taught New Testament at San Francisco Theological Seminary since 1973, since 1984 as full professor. Previously she taught at the School of Theology in Claremont and at Appalachian University, Boone, North Carolina. She has been awarded Woodrow Wilson, Fulbright, Layne Archaeological, and Association of Theological Schools Research Fellowships for study in Germany, Israel, and the United States. She spent the fall of 1987 in Nanjing, China, doing research on the biblical interpretation of the Chinese Christian Three-Self Movement and returned there for further study in the spring of 1989.

Dr. Wire has written on Pauline theology, on the gospel miracle stories, on economics and class origins in biblical and early Christian literature, and on ancient women's asceticism, Corinthian women prophets, and feminist theological reconstruction. Her writings include *The Parable Is a Mirror*, written in 1983 for the Presbyterian Church in the United States and the United Presbyterian Church (USA), and *The Corinthian Women Prophets: A Reconstruction through Paul's Rhetoric* (Minneapolis: Fortress, 1990). She served on the Presbyterian General Assembly Committee for writing a Brief Statement of the Reformed Faith.